Cover:
<!-- HTML Credit Code for Can Stock Photo -->
<a href="https://www.canstockphoto.com">(c) Can Stock Photo / yuriyzhuravov</a>

MEMORIES

Marianne Pilgrim Davidson

PTP
PTP Book Division
Arizona

PTP Book Division
Imprint of Saguaro Books, LLC
16845 E. Avenue of the Fountains, Ste. 325
Fountain Hills, AZ 85268
www.ptpbookdivision.com

ISBN: 978-1-0881-3140-4
Library of Congress Cataloging Number
LCCN: 2021949848
Printed in the United States of America
First Edition

Dedication

I dedicate this book to all the women in my family past, present and future.

Chapter 1

My name is Ann and my first memory is of the apartment with the kitchen in the middle between the living room and the bedroom on the second floor above a funeral parlor. I couldn't have been more than four years old.

The doorbell rang and I ran into the bedroom and my sister ran into the living room so the doctor couldn't get us. We knew the doctor was coming, my mother had told us. The doctor and my mother sat in the kitchen and waited for us to come out. I decided to go into the living room where my sister was and that's when the doctor caught me crossing the kitchen. I guess he gave me a needle or something. Those were the days when doctors made house calls.

Next memory was still in that apartment, but looking out the kitchen window at my father and a policeman down in the street with my father's clothes lying around him and my mother running back and forth throwing my father's clothes out the window. Then she sat down and cried and I didn't know what to do. We were left alone—my mother, me and my sister.

We were in the apartment alone with my mother for a few months. A man, I guess the landlord, started coming to the door, telling us we would have to move out. He came to the door often to tell us to move out. My mother pleaded, she didn't know where to go and to give her more time. We still had to go.

I remember going down to the basement where the furnace was and my mother putting more coal in the furnace so the building would have heat. She had to take us down there with her because we were too young to be left alone. It was scary down in the basement with the big old furnace and the long hallway to get to it. She got a break on the rent for putting coal in the furnace.

There was a long stairway against the wall going up to the apartment. My father once dropped us off after a visit. I remember having a candlelight dinner with him and a woman. When he brought us home, my sister and I were on the platform in the middle of the open stairway. My father was on the bottom floor and my mother was on the top of the stairway, they were screaming at each other and my father said to me and my sister, "Come here to me." My mother said, "Come here to me." My sister and I just stood there. My mother came down the stairs to where we were and took us by the hand up to the apartment.

She needed money to pay the bills. Our father didn't send her child support or alimony. He was one of these deadbeat dads as they are called today. In those days there were no computers. It was easy for someone to get lost and not have to be hauled into court and made to pay child support and alimony. At one point, the courts forced my paternal grandfather to pay the child support and alimony for his son. Yes, in those days the courts did that. Unfortunately, my grandfather died six months after starting to pay us then we were left with nothing again.

My father sent us ice skates and my mother said what are we going to do with them? I can't afford to take you ice skating. My mother told us to write a thank you to our father and ask him for some money for our dental bill.

Oh the dentist, he would drill your cavities without Novocain. Yes, that's what they did in those days. It was terribly painful. I hated going to the dentist. Somehow, my mother paid the dental bill.

Years later, my father sent us two Mexican dolls, a boy and a girl. I kept them in my drawer for years. I never played with them. I just looked at them every once in a while. They were the only things I received from my father in years so I wanted to keep them. Again my mother said to write him a thank you and ask for money to pay the bills.

One Christmas, my Uncle Tommy came to pick me and my sister up to go to his house. He had an armful of presents and my sister and me on either side of him. When we got outside, my father came up to him and said he was taking us for Christmas. My uncle at first said OK but then added all our cousins, aunts, uncles and grandma were back at his house waiting to see us. They would be disappointed if we didn't go.

I didn't want to go with my father; I wanted to go with my uncle. I don't know if anyone asked us but my father let us go with my uncle. I can't remember seeing my father again until I was eighteen.

Then there was the house with many kids and a screaming woman. We had a room off the kitchen. When we got there, my mother told me to go look out the window. I remember being afraid to walk through the kitchen because the woman would always be screaming.

The father would come home when we were all sitting around watching TV. He would roughhouse with his kids—messing their hair, hugging, kissing and throwing them up in the air. I would watch. They seemed to really enjoy each other and I saw how fathers interacted with their children. It did make me miss my father. It also gave me a look into how middle-class families behave and the role the father played in the intact family.

We started school early. We were born on December 28. The cutoff date was December 1 to enter kindergarten. My mother somehow got us into school that year. She needed to go to work and needed us in school so she could do that.

First of all, you should be five when you enter kindergarten. If you are a middle-class child, your parents keep you at home another year and start you when you are six. Or they put you in private school so you could start when you were five and not a year younger than the other students. That is not the case in lower-class families. They need to put their children in school as soon as possible so they are free to go to work.

In New York, the cut off was December 1, which was a big disadvantage to the children whose birthdays were after September. If we were born on December 1, we would have had a great disadvantage being the youngest in the class. To be put in when our birthday was December 28 was a disadvantage even greater.

We were too young to start school. Plus, we came from a broken home. We had the psychological disadvantage of that. We had no money so we had that disadvantage, too. It was no surprise we were always in the lowest reading group. Plus, we were too young to grasp certain fundamentals and missed understanding the foundation of certain learning concepts. Also, we were part of the baby boomers. There were so many children; therefore, no one had time to give individual help to students who needed it.

There is a saying: "Your IQ is as high as your father's salary". That is partially true. If your father is making money you will have all the advantages of tutors or whatever else, you need to succeed in school.

When we went to school, my mother would lean out the window and tell us when to cross the street to go to kindergarten. I remember never getting the big chairs in kindergarten when the teacher told us to go get our chairs. She was an older woman. I remember we mixed cream into butter and we all got a chance mixing the cream.

I walked to school. One time, I walked to school in the rain and when I got there I was soaked. The nun took off my shoes and socks and wrapped my feet in a blanket. It felt good but I was so embarrassed by the attention I could hardly keep the blanket on. I was ashamed of who I was. I didn't feel worthy of her attention. I was a poor child from a broken home. *What right do I have to get such attention.*

We stopped living with friends and moved to a cold flat. There was only a stove in the kitchen to keep us warm. My mother painted the apartment. The neighbor said she shouldn't have bothered painting the front rooms. We weren't going to use them when it got cold. We would only be in the kitchen and the room off the kitchen. She was right—as soon as it got cold we stayed in those two rooms.

We found a mouse in the closet in the mousetrap. I screamed and screamed when my mother used the broom to get rid of it. I just remember much screaming. My mother also cut our hair short in that cold flat. She said it was easier to keep. I remember coloring on the floor by the stove and asking my mother if I wrote any letters. She hardly had time to look at what I was doing. She was so busy trying to keep everything together.

There were many Irish girls living in the apartment building and they would hit and say mean things. I remember telling my mother they were mean and she said don't play with them. So I would run past them while they yelled things at me to get into the apartment. Soon it was cold and they weren't outside anymore.

I remember sitting on a chair in the room off the kitchen crying and wailing. My mother was at work and she left me and my sister alone. I cried and wailed for a few hours. I knew then I had to accept that I would have to work and do things for myself, if I wanted to survive. I decided that day, after crying and wailing for a few hours, I would accept what I was given and be strong and depend on myself if I wanted anything. My mother told me a neighbor said I'd been wailing and crying for hours. Did I do that? I said, "No."

My mother had to go to work so she left us with babysitters. One time, she left us with a family whose daughter had polio. Her legs were so skinny. They told me to sit next to her on the bench at the table, so I did but I was afraid I was going to get polio. Then my mother asked me if I was afraid I would get polio and I said, "Yes." She didn't take us there anymore. A few years later, in school, they lined all the kids up and gave us a polio shot. The next two times we had to eat a sugar cube, with the vaccine in it.

There was a nice little old lady babysitter who would put us in the carriage and take us for walks, she would tell us to close our eyes so the dirt wouldn't get in them when the wind blew. I liked her. One time, her friend came over and drew a picture of a girl with a round mouth for me. I liked the picture. I remember the friend saying poor little things. I guess she felt sorry for us with no father.

She discovered that my sister and I needed glasses and told my mother we may need glasses. In those days, young children didn't get glasses. When we started school then we got glasses. Someone said it was because we were put in incubators when we were first born. Twins usually had a low birth weight, I was about 4 lbs. and so was my sister when we were born. So they put us in incubators and the blowing of the air affected our eyesight, so they say; who knows.

We locked a young girl babysitter outside the apartment, once. I was afraid when I did it. I guess we eventually let her in. I told my mother I wanted to babysit myself but I really was afraid to do that. The young girl never came back.

My mother got sick in the cold flat, probably the flu, my aunt and uncle came then. My aunt said she would clean the apartment but she never did. We stayed with my aunt and uncle a few days until my mother was well. I was afraid when my mother was sick, I didn't know what would happen to me. In a few days, we were allowed to go back to the cold flat and my mother was able to take care of us. I was so happy to be back with my mother.

Some women from the welfare department came when my mother was at work to see us in the cold flat. My mother had piled clothes on the TV to try to hide it. We were afraid the welfare department would take our TV away; but the women looked at the clothes then pushed some of them away. I don't know what she concluded but soon we moved into the Projects.

Chapter 2

Those years in the Projects were the happiest years of my childhood. My mother used to tell us stories of Petunia and Geranium. Two little girl flowers, I guess my sister and I were the two flowers. She would fold little birds out of paper and their wings would move and look like they were flying. We would go visit cousin Mary in Hoboken, take the ferry over then climb the stairs to the top floor apartment and have a great Italian dinner. I guess my mother had fewer money problems, or, at least, we had a decent place to live because we seemed to go places and have fun.

We had a first-floor apartment in the Projects—two bedrooms, kitchen, living room, bathroom and heat. Heat was the most wonderful thing about the Projects. My sister and I shared a room with one dresser and a closet. I remember my sister tried to convince me to take the two bottom drawers of the dresser. Finally, we compromised, and she got the top drawer and I got the second and the third drawer and she got the bottom drawer.

Our bedroom window was right over some work area and, in the summer, the noisy workmen would wake us up early in the morning. We were alone and too afraid to tell them they were loud. My mother worked during the summer making sweaters in the sweatshops of Brooklyn. She left early in the morning before we got up. We really didn't go anywhere; we just stayed in the apartment, maybe played hopscotch in the front of the building. Mostly we watched TV.

My mother made a list of things we could do, one summer. On one day, she scheduled us to go to the library, the next day to the local school for the summer program, another day at the pool. We found walking to the library a long, hot walk so after a while we stopped going. The school program was held in the hot old school. It was cooler and more pleasant to stay at home. The local pool was so crowded all you did was get splashed and there was not enough room to even try to swim. Plus, there were rumors polio was transmitted through pools. So we went once to the pool and never went again.

I don't remember how we made friends with Cookie and Judy, the two Jewish girls who lived on the second floor but we did and we had the best time together. We played hopscotch and we would all sit around the TV and watch Walt Disney on Sunday nights. No one was allowed to talk. The show was too important.

Their mother was nice, she was a secretary and she had a bad back. Their father would walk around the apartment in his robe; their older brother wasn't around much. They would call me to their apartment on Friday nights to turn on the lights or the TV. The mother would put a towel over her head and say prayers. They would give me matzo with salt and butter.

Cookie and Judy were smarter than my sister and me. They never said anything about it but we all knew. They didn't go to school on Friday but they went a half day on Sunday. They would look at my notebook and tell me what to write.

Just once the father, who never said anything, said to me spell Catholic, I couldn't and then he said to Judy spell Jew and she did. I ran down stairs to my apartment. I was ashamed of my ignorance.

I was a better hopscotch player than Cookie or Judy. I could jump the squares better than either of them. We would comb each other's hair. Talk about movies and records. I remember Cookie telling us about the movie *Psycho,* which a friend of hers had seen. Years after, when I did see it, I wasn't disappointed; it was scary, just as Cookie had described.

We did go to the movies. Our mother would give us money to go to the movies on Saturday morning, so she could go food shopping and do housework. I did see many movies. We paid the children's prices. One time, my sister had to go home and get her birth certificate to prove her age so we could pay the children's price.

Every penny counted but I never saw my mother use coupons. I don't know if they had coupons in those days. I don't think she shopped at discount stores. At one point, someone told her where to find some discount stores. She went and was surprised at the low prices.

The welfare department gave us some powdered milk and some pancake mix but my mother never went back to get it again. We only went once for the free toys at Christmas. I guess my mother didn't believe in getting something for nothing or, maybe, she didn't want to take charity. Whatever the reason, I don't remember doing any of that in my childhood.

Judy, at one point had enough money to buy a record. She bought *Paper Tiger* by Fabian then she didn't like it. I asked her if she had heard it before she bought it. She only heard the ending. You had to be very careful when you bought something, as you were going to have to live with the decision whether you liked it or not. What you had, especially toys were very precious. You didn't get another if it broke, if it wasn't what you expected, you lost it or let someone steal it.

I brought one of my books to school one time. Someone stole it. I told the teacher and she had everyone look in the school bag of the person next to them but no one saw it. I went home without my book and my mother couldn't buy me a new one. I never took anything to school again. The few toys I had were very precious. I learned very young to protect them.

When we got a little older, we started to go with Cookie and Judy to Brighton Beach. We would meet Jewish boys there. We were about ten or eleven. The girls would get on the boys' shoulders, in the water, and try to push the other girl off the boy's shoulder. It was a great game. We would get a cherry cheese knish on the way to the beach, which was the most delicious thing I had ever tasted. It was fun talking to the boys. I don't think they knew I wasn't Jewish. I started writing to one of the boys when summer was over but that fizzled, quickly.

When my sister and I were on the beach alone, it got dark and stormy. We went into the water anyway and some man came running at us telling us to get out of the water, it was lightning. We didn't know how dangerous the beach could be in a lightning storm. Thank goodness there was someone there who cared enough to tell us. We went home on the subway with wet bathing suits. When children do things by themselves, one has to hope there are adults around who will help them. Children are ignorant of many dangers and they need protection.

As we got older, my mother did try to introduce us to music. Cookie and Judy had a piano in their apartment and our parents found a piano teacher who could give us group lessons. Because we didn't have a piano, we got a cardboard piano keyboard on which to practice. This was not a great incentive to practice. We had the lessons upstairs in Cookie and Judy's apartment where the piano was. Judy did really well because she could practice on her piano. I did terribly and didn't take piano lessons for very long. The cardboard piano didn't give me much incentive to learn; but then again, I don't think I had the talent for it because as an adult I tried to take lessons using a regular keyboard and I still couldn't play.

There was a Spanish family who lived across the hall from us. They were sweet and nice. The older girls would babysit us when my mother went out. They were kind and gentle and seemed to genuinely care. Sometimes we went to their apartment after school and they would help us drink the milk my mother left for us. Even the older brothers would encourage us. Regular milk was considered really good for children at that time. No one knew about dairy allergies.

When my mother left us at my cousins' house, my cousins and I were not getting along. They told Karen, their little sister, to hit me. I ran home but I couldn't get into my apartment so I went to the Spanish family's apartment and they let me in theirs. Later that night, my cousin came with a visiting cousin from New Jersey to get me. They said my aunt and uncle wanted me to come back with them and they took my cousin from New Jersey to show me they really were here. I refused to go and asked the Spanish family if I could sleep over in their apartment that night. They nodded yes. Then about an hour later my uncle came and I did go back with him.

My aunt and uncle lived near us so I saw my three cousins often. When my Uncle Tommy, Aunt Kay and my three cousins were over at our house, we were all playing and Karen wanted my doll. I told her no. She started crying and told her parents. Gala came up to me and told me to let Karen have my doll because she would only play with it for a while then would give it back. I said 'no'. I was sick of catering to Karen and giving my dolls to other kids. Karen kept crying, my uncle came and asked me to give her the doll and I said 'no'. Then my uncle left and came back a little while later with a new doll for Karen. Everyone looked at me as if I done something wrong. Until this day, I'm torn about whether or not I did something wrong.

I watch kids and see, many times, kids don't want to share their toys. Then I see parents making them share their toy. Who is right, is there a right? When I had my own children I made my son share his toy, one time. He started crying and looked at me with a look that said how could you do this to me. The other kid was happy and now my son was crying. I felt as if I had betrayed my own child and never made him share a toy again. I decided my first job was to make my child happy, not make someone else's child happy.

When I was a child living in the Projects we were robbed. You would think robbers would go to an upscale neighborhood and rob. Yet, for whatever reason, they stayed in their neighborhood and robbed the poor. One night, I heard a terrible scream, my sister heard it too. We got up and went to my mother's bedroom but she wasn't there. We looked around the apartment but she wasn't anywhere. We went to the Spanish neighbors and asked them if she was there and she wasn't. They had heard the scream too.

Then we heard my mother outside and we all went to the main door and opened it to look out. There was my mother walking toward the building crying and screaming. There had been a black man in the apartment and he took her pocketbook. She had run after him.

I was just happy to see she was safe. The Spanish neighbors helped her in the apartment and called the police. She said she had heard the bird in the kitchen chirping and chirping. So she went into the kitchen to see what the matter was and there was a black man in the kitchen.

When he saw her, he grabbed her pocketbook off the kitchen table and ran out. My mother, in her fright had run after him; but, thankfully, came to her senses and came back to the apartment. The police arrived and there were many people taking statements. They said he probably climbed in through the window, we were on the ground floor, after all.

Eventually, they did find my mother's pocketbook in the bushes near the apartment. The money was gone. My mother was asked about it for a good long time by her family and friends. They all wanted to know why she ran after him. She didn't know why. I guess in your fright you never know what you are going to do.

Life went on and holidays came. At Halloween, we wanted to dress up and go trick or treating. My mother worked until about 6 o'clock in the evening, so we would be by ourselves until she got home. On Halloween, she told us to dress up in her old dresses. A bunch of kids were outside cutting holes in sheets to make a ghost costume. One of them put a sheet over my head and cut a hole for the eyes, poking me in the eye with the scissors. Luckily, it was a round edge scissors. Children need adult supervision.

We didn't get much when we knocked on people's doors. Most people weren't home. What we did get was a mean old man running out of his apartment yelling at us. We ran outside and he ran after us screaming, picking up stones and throwing them at us. After that, my sister wanted to go home so we did. I think we only went trick or treating once, or maybe twice.

What I do remember, which was nice about Halloween was my mother would buy a Halloween cake with charms in it. So, whatever piece we got, we'd get a charm. We would wait for my mother to come home with the cake. I remember one rainy Halloween when my mother was really late; we got very worried and scared. My cousins were with us and all of us were frightened. Minnie, the next-door neighbor, stayed with us until Mother got home. We all got some cake and that's how we spent Halloween. We have a picture of us all at Halloween around the table eating the cake. I don't know where that picture is but I still see it in my mind. I don't know who could have taken it. Maybe my aunt or uncle had a camera. We didn't have a camera.

Minnie would kind of look after us in the summer when my mother worked and we were home alone all day. Most days we never saw Minnie. One time, we were playing with the ants and the caterpillars in front of our building, while they were eating each other. Minnie came out with a big pot of hot water and washed them away then she went back to her apartment.

She also looked out her window and yelled at me to stop when I was skating and I decided to skate on the handrail that goes up the ramp. I climbed the gate and the ramp with my skates hooked up to the edge of the handrail. I think my sister told her because I was going high and she was afraid I would fall. My skates were pretty secure between the handrail and the concrete but Minnie told me to get down, anyway.

At one point, Minnie said she wanted to talk to me. I went into her apartment and when we were alone she said, why are you jealous of your sister? I was really surprised she would ask me such a thing. I told her I'm not jealous of my sister. She said yes you are. I said no I'm not and this went on for a while. I kept saying "No I'm not" and she kept saying, "Yes you are". Finally, I wanted to go out and play and have this over with, so I said, "OK yes I am. Can I go now?"

She let me go. I didn't know why Minnie had said this. It was all new to me but, a few weeks later, my mother said you are jealous of your sister. I said I wasn't and she said I know you are because you told Minnie you were. So I told her how Minnie kept telling me I was jealous of my sister and I kept saying I wasn't until I wanted to go and play. Then I just said I was so I could leave. My mother just shook her head. I had no idea how they came up with this.

My sister and I would skate a lot, especially when we got home from school until my mother came home. I remember we skated way into late autumn until it got too cold to stay out for very long. We would put our skates on with the skate key but we never were able to make them tight enough. Sometimes we would ask a man to tighten them for us so they would stay on longer.

One day, my mother came home from work while we were out skating. She told us to come in. We told her we didn't want to. She seemed really annoyed so, in a little while, I went in and my sister stayed out. When I got in the apartment my mother started beating me to a point of really hurting me. I tried to hide under the kitchen table but she got me anyway. I just was screaming and screaming. Minnie knocked on the door and calmed my mother down and wanted to see me.

I was crying and sobbing but I guess I was OK. Minnie left and my mother said to me, see what you did. I didn't quite understand what I did. I was confused. My sister then came in and my mother hit her on the behind but that was it. The next day, walking to school, my side hurt but it felt better in a few days.

Single mothers are under much pressure, especially the poor ones. At that time, there were no organizations one could go to for support. Single mothers were on their own.

My mother had to work, take care of the house and us. We were left alone a lot. My sister and I would fight, especially in the summer, when we were home all day by ourselves. We would chase each other around the apartment with brooms and hit each other with them, hopefully across the face. We sometimes accomplished that.

When I was walking home from school by myself, one day, I don't know why I wasn't with my sister. There were a bunch of black girls who I had to pass to get home. When I passed them, one of them told me to open my month. I knew she was going to put whatever she had in her hand in my mouth. I think she had some kind of bug. I put my hand over my mouth and ran. The black girls couldn't keep up with me. Soon I was a safe distance from them and I got home. You had to watch out if you were alone. I learned to watch where I was going and maybe turn around or go another way, if I saw something I didn't think was safe.

I remember one summer day, we were outside playing, when someone came with a camera and told all the kids to sit on the steps so they could take a picture. I ran inside; I was afraid. Then I thought it was my father, who hired them to take pictures of all the kids to find us. I felt I should have taken the picture. I guess I still missed him and hoped he would come back to us. That never happened. I had learned to be afraid of strangers and learn to run inside for protection. I became afraid of anything that was strange or new. I felt I had to be very cautious. I had to protect myself; no one was going to do it for me. If I got into trouble, I had to get out of it myself.

During the summer there were one or two flowers that would grow in the bushes of the Projects. All the kids would crowd around if they found a flower and look at it. It was a yellow round fuzzy flower. One time, my sister picked it real fast and ran into the house. She put it in a little water and thought about what she had. It was just a dandelion but that's what kids in the Project thought were pretty flowers. They were the only flowers we ever saw.

Chapter 3

My mother and grandmother had fought about my mother staying married to my father. My mother kept going back to my father even after he hit her, cheated on her and didn't work. My grandmother finally told her to not ask her for help anymore, if she was going to stay with him. So they didn't talk for years.

In time, my mother and grandmother were talking to each other again and we would go over to her house on Long Island. My grandmother invited me and my sister to go out to her house on Long Island for a week.

My grandmother tried to entertain us, I remember she made Yorkshire pudding once and she took us food shopping with her. She took us somewhere where she wouldn't tell us where she was going and left us in the car while she went in. I also remember my grandmother telling me to have a good time while I was young; really telling me to have a good time when I was young, emotionally.

She had a horrible time when she was young. Her father had put a knife to her throat and told her she had to marry a thirty-two-year-old man. She was sixteen when she married him. When she took her marriage vows, she told God she didn't want to marry him and she didn't mean her vows of marriage. She had four children with him. My mother was the oldest then her brother Joe, her sister Rose and her brother Tommy, which was my Uncle Tommy.

When she was in the hospital giving birth to one of the babies, her husband sold the house in which they lived. When she got out of the hospital, he brought her to the new house, a much smaller, run-down house in Camden, New Jersey. He told her it would be a boarding house and she would take care of boarders. In those days, women weren't allowed to own property.

My grandmother did own a house in Italy because she inherited it. It was given to her by her grandmother when she died. Her older uncle was living in it. My grandmother's husband made her sign the house over to him and he put his family in Italy in it. He kicked her old uncle out. She told the story of how the uncle wrote her a letter telling her how devastated he was that in his old age he had to leave the house he'd lived in all his life.

My grandmother tried to leave her husband. She tried leaving with the four children but he found her and made her go back with him. She had no money and was just about surviving with the four children. The second time, she left with a man who had been a boarder in the house. She left the children behind. That was the only way she could leave him. The children were put in an orphanage. My mother and Tommy were put in one orphanage Joe and Rose in another.

When my grandmother settled in NY, she came back and got my mother and Tommy from their orphanage but she didn't know in what orphanage Joe and Rose were. She couldn't find them so they stayed in Camden and my mother and Tommy went to New York with their mother and her second husband.

My Uncle Tommy was only about two when she got him from the orphanage. She told the story of a kind nurse sneaking my Uncle Tommy out of the orphanage one night and giving him to her in just a blanket. On the train to New York, he sang *It ain't going to rain no more, no more*. He was so happy to be with his mother.

About thirty years later, my mother was reunited with her sister Rose and brother Joe by a chance meeting. A cousin lived in New Jersey and knew my mother. The cousin worked in a vitamin store. One day, a woman came into the store, who looked much the same as my mother. The cousin asked her name and sure enough, it was Rose, the long-lost sister of my mother. We then went to visit her. Joe had died by then.

My grandmother had two more children, Dave and Lucy, with her second husband. Then her second husband was killed by a truck when he was crossing the street. The insurance company and her lawyer cheated her out of insurance money. Her lawyer gave her fifty dollars for her second husband's death and kept the rest for himself. She had no money to fight him so she was left a widow, with four children to support.

Until this day, I'm wary of insurance companies. I'm not going to say I distrust lawyers, because my daughter became a lawyer. I had a few experiences with insurance companies and I feel they will try to get out of paying you. I even had to get a lawyer once to be paid by an insurance company. Thank God, I had the intelligence to fight them. I found a lawyer who took money only when he won the case. He did win this one.

My grandmother went to the Roman Catholic Church and asked for money and the priest told her he didn't know her, he had never seen her at church and refused to give her anything. She never went to church after that. My mother had to leave school after eighth grade to work to bring in money to put food on the table. My grandmother worked too. She managed to bring them up but she never did get back to New Jersey to get Rose and Joe.

Memories

When her children were grown, she married her third husband and they went to live on Long Island in a little house on a half-acre of land. The third husband was the only grandfather I ever knew. He didn't do much, didn't say much. So it was fine.

We all went to visit my grandmother at her house on Long Island. Sometimes, my sister and I would stay with her for a week or so. When we were at my grandmother's house, my sister and I still fought. I threw a shoe at her and it hit the glass in the storm door and broke it. My step-grandfather had to change it to the screen. When my mother came to pick us up, she was upset that we had fought so much.

Sometimes, my grandmother had my cousins and us over—all four of us at the same time, me, my sister, Gala and Sherry. All we did was fight. We had nothing else to do. No toys, we weren't taken anywhere or maybe we went to a drive-in movie one night.

I remember my grandmother had some ex-lax and we wanted some because it tasted like chocolate so she gave us all some. The next day it was all of us and one bathroom. What a situation that was.

Sometimes we would all go out to my grandmother's house in Long Island, especially during the summer; my mother, stepfather, Uncle Tommy, Aunt Kay, Gala, Sherry and Karen. Sometimes we would all stay overnight in the little two-bedroom house. We kids would sleep with blankets on the floor. The lucky one would get to sleep on a lawn chair. They were fun weekends. We would go to a drive-in movie at night. I loved that. I saw the movie *Some Like It Hot*. It was a great movie. I was able to see the Big Dipper in the sky because it was so dark out there.

My uncle would teach us all how to ride bikes on two old bikes we found in the garage. The bikes were too big for us. We had to get on a box to jump on and they were boy's bikes with the bar, so it was not easy. I remember my uncle holding the back of the bike and pushing us and letting go. Of course, most of the time we would wind up falling to the ground but, eventually, we learned to ride a bike.

We also went to the beach. I remember when my stepfather said I couldn't go to the beach. I don't remember what I did but he decided to punish me by not taking me to the beach. They all left, leaving me with my grandmother. A little while later, my Uncle Tommy and Aunt Kay arrived with Gala, Sherry and Karen and decided to go to the beach. They took me with them.

They did find my mother, stepfather, and sister at the beach. My stepfather was mad they had taken me. My mother finally told him there was nothing she could do. I was there and that was that.

One weekend, we were over at my grandmother's house and it was Sunday. I wanted to go to Mass. I asked if someone could drive me. No one wanted to drive me. So I asked how to get to the church and I would walk. Catholic schools taught me that you had to go to Mass on Sunday or it was a mortal sin. I wanted to go to Mass.

So I set out to walk to church. I had walked a little way when a car with a couple pulled up next to me and asked me where I was going. I told them I was going to church. So they asked what church and I told them the Roman Catholic Church. They said they could drive me there.

I got into the car. We drove quite a way; I don't think I would have been able to walk that far. We got to the church and I went to Mass with the couple. After Mass was over, they said they would drive me home and they did.

They left me off at the back of my grandmother's house. I think the woman wanted to walk me to the door but the man said just leave her here. When I went into my grandmother's house, no one believed I had gone to church. My grandmother said I was just sitting in the bushes. My mother seemed a little upset that I had gone by myself but I was back and that was the important thing.

I used to go to church on Sunday; this is what I learned in Catholic school. When we lived in Forest Hills, one of the neighbors gave me a little handkerchief because I went to church every Sunday by myself.

Later in life, I found out from my sister, she and my mother saw it as being defiant and I was being difficult, going to church, even if no one wanted to drive me. They felt I should have stayed home and not aggravated anyone. I still don't know what was right.

Chapter 4

When Thanksgiving came, we would go to the Thanksgiving day parade, we went to it every year. My Aunt Kay would stay home and cook the Thanksgiving dinner and my mother would take me, my sister and my two cousins Gala and Sherry to the Macy's Thanksgiving parade. We did this for years. It was wonderful. My mother would tell us to ask the people if we could get up front and we did. We had a great view of the parade.

One year my cousin Sherry had to go to the bathroom and my mother asked her if she knew where to go and she said yes; but of course she didn't so in a little while my mother told us we had to go find Sherry. We left our front row place and went looking for Sherry. I could see my mother was worried and she finally asked a police officer. They took us to the police station and sure enough there was Sherry. She had one of those dolls on a stick and policemen all around her playing and making her feel comfortable, watching the parade on TV.

We did have some good times on those Thanksgivings. My Aunt Kay was a great cook. It was wonderful to be out in the chilled air, watching the parade then coming home to a wonderful Thanksgiving dinner. My aunt and uncle lived on the top floor of a third story walk up apartment building. It was a railroad room apartment in an old building. Supposedly apartments were hard to find after the war and that's the only one they could find they could afford.

At Christmas my mother would buy a real tree. We would carry it home. I remember my mother counting her dollar bills over and over because she thought she got cheated out of a dollar. She finally realized she didn't.

Cookie and Judy would come down and decorate the tree with us. When Cookie broke one of the ornaments, my mother told her it was OK but she went upstairs anyway. When she left we all felt bad.

We also baked Christmas cookies and iced them with red, green and yellow icing. Cookie and Judy would do that with us. Our cousins Gala and Sherry, who only lived about three blocks away, would come too. My mother told them they could take home whatever they decorated and Gala just smeared icing on many cookies so she could take as many as she could home.

My mother would take us to Macy's on 34th street to look at the Christmas window display. Then we would pick a toy at Macy's for Christmas. I always picked a doll. My mother would put our choice on layaway and we always got it in time for Christmas.

I had gotten a ballet toe dancing doll with joints that would move, one Christmas. She was made out of plastic but her head was rubber. I played with her all the time. Her head ripped and her hair fell out. My mother took her to a factory and got me a new doll but I was so upset because her face wasn't the face of my doll. We actually took a taxi back to the factory and got her head back. We kept the new body. My mother sewed yarn hair on her and stitched up her head so it would stay on the body.

We would go to Radio City Christmas Spectacular waiting in line outside for hours, freezing in the cold and finally getting in; we saw a movie then the show. I loved the show. It was spectacular. It was magical. There is nothing like Radio City at Christmas.

My mother also brought us to Broadway plays. She was a member of the Eastern Stars and they would get group rate tickets to plays on Broadway. She brought us to see our first play it was "Gypsy" with Ethel Merman. I loved it. I was hooked on Broadway, Radio City and all the theaters in Manhattan.

We had Christmas Eve at our house, sometimes. I remember my Aunt Lucy calling out the names on the presents. One Christmas, my doll present was the last one called. I remember how hard it was to be patient and wait. I got presents from my Aunt Kay and Uncle Tommy, my Aunt Yolanda and Uncle Davie.

One time, my Aunt Yolanda and Uncle Davey gave me and my sister a sled. There were no hills in the Projects so we would just push it on the sidewalk we soon got tired of that. My cousin Sherry came over to play with it.

My grandmother would give us all PJs for Christmas. The four of us, my sister, Gala and Sherry, were at her house one Christmas. We were in the bedroom pretending to be asleep and we heard the doorbell ring and the delivery man bringing presents; but I don't remember getting presents. We used to sleep together in twin beds. It was very uncomfortable sleeping with my cousin Sherry. She would kick in her sleep.

My mother would buy aprons for the women in the family for Christmas and colored pencil drawing kits for the kids. She gave us a little extra money one year to buy aprons and we spent the extra money on candy. My sister told me my mother had given us extra money to see if we would buy her something for Christmas but we had already bought the candy.

That Christmas, my Aunt Lucy wrapped up a handkerchief and told me and my sister to give it to my mother. My mother was so happy Until she opened the package and saw only a handkerchief. I had hurt my mother without even knowing it.

Memories

After the Christmas Holidays, it was a dreary winter. Sometimes my cousins would come to our house after school and we would all be alone in our apartment. Gala punched me in the head when she was looking in the door key of our apartment. I thought she looked funny doing that so I touched her head and she hauled off and punched me in the head. She once fought with my sister about who would get the root beer lollipop the dry cleaner man had given us. They were pulling each other's hair. The man said "I don't know what happened. I gave them each a lollipop and they started to fight".

Unattended kids were constantly fighting in the Projects. A black girl was fighting with my sister and I just watched. I guess my sister was winning. A boy once hit me in the eye with a stick. My cousin Sherry said "Let's get him" and we found him and chased him straight to his apartment. His mother came out and wanted to know what we were doing. We told her what he did to my eye and she gave my eye a good look. Some kids were seriously hurt, luckily I never was.

Easter came and we did get a new dress and a new coat. We even have some pictures of us at Easter with my cousins. Sometimes we would go out to my grandmother's house for Easter. We would have the wheat pies and the sausage pies Italians made for Easter. My mother would make the wheat pie from scratch. She would buy all the fresh ingredients from the local Italian stores in Brooklyn. I would love them.

I remember wanting cupcakes and my sister and I looked for any money around the house. We got up a little money and we went to the bakery with the mean man behind the counter and bought cupcakes. He gave us stale hard cupcakes we couldn't even eat. I guess that was one of the reasons why we started making our own cakes and sweet things. He went out of business.

I sent away for a free bread recipe book and I started to make bread. I stayed home from school so I could make the bread, it had to rise. I made Sally Lynn bread. We all enjoyed the homemade bread.

Some nice women made chocolate pudding for us kids and I wouldn't eat it. She asked me why and I said I didn't like the skin on it. She took the skin off and I loved chocolate pudding from then on. We cooked chocolate pudding often.

My mother started making chocolate cream pie, she made the real pie crust, not the graham cracker kind, then she made the cooked MT Fine chocolate pudding and she beat up the heavy cream into real whipped cream. It was delicious. It's still my favorite dessert.

My mother would take us to the automat where they would have food in little windows so you could pick what you wanted. I would always pick the chocolate cream pie. I put my money in and the little door would open and there would be my pie. It wasn't as good as my mother's, though.

Chapter 5

Children, especially in their elementary years are easily influenced. I remember I wanted to be a nun; mostly because I was around nuns. They were my teachers, so I was used to them. They were adults and I wanted to please the adults. I needed their approval and their help to survive. Parents are especially influential in their child's life. Children want to please their parents at all costs.

If you put a child in a Catholic school, they will learn the Catholic ways and think that's the way of life. The Nazis put children in schools and taught them their ways and that's what the children believed and learned. Any government knows they have to get control of the youth of the country. It doesn't have to be right or wrong, children will learn and believe it's the right way of life. If the adults around them want them to learn and believe in these things, that's what the child will believe. It takes many years, if ever, to unlearn some of the concepts you learn as a child. These concepts get ingrained in your young mind and they stay there.

In my elementary school years, I spent half my time in Catholic school and half my time in public school. Both have good and bad points. After Catholic school, I had to unlearn some of the philosophy they taught. Some of the Catholic school ideas just didn't work in the real world, especially in the working world.

First you had to get rid of the idea that everyone was Christian. Everyone doesn't think like a Catholic. Everyone wasn't kind and thoughtful, especially in the workplace. Being humble didn't work when you were working. You had to be a little aggressive and say it was your idea.

In real life, the Catholic ways seemed to keep women submissive. They taught a good Christian woman, didn't use birth control, didn't get divorced, brought her children up Catholic and was a good, obedient wife. Love, honor and obey were the marriage vows. These were some of the things I saw as a child that didn't seem to work. Women stayed married to men who beat them, had children they couldn't afford and had to obey men that just did stupid things. This was the rule of poverty and suppression of women.

People weren't so narrow-minded about sex either. Of course, you learned in Catholic school no sex before marriage. It was almost like saying leave the girl ignorant about sex so her husband had control over what she would learn and be told about sex. He was in control of the sex life. He could tell her anything and she would believe it because she had no sexual experience.

In the working world at that time it was a man's world. The Catholic rules about boys and girls and sex just weren't going on in the real world. It was a shock to me when I got my first job and saw what happened at the office parties. Married men and women didn't act married. Girls were having sex before they were married.

Mostly it was this humble, meek-shall-inherit-the-earth attitude that I had to unlearn. If you were meek you just got pushed aside, especially in New York. You had to be a go-getter and sell yourself. You couldn't go to a job interview with a meek attitude. You had to go to a job interview with an attitude that I am good and I can do the job for you. I think, at least in public school, I didn't have to unlearn too much of the philosophy that they taught. They really didn't teach too many morals.

We went to PS 36, there were many kids in an old building. At that time, there would be bomb drills. The teacher would tell all the students to get under their desks and put their hands over their heads. Looking back, it was really stupid. What good would going under your desk do if there was really an atomic bomb? After a while, that stopped and fire drills began. Many schools had fires and children were burned to death because they didn't know how to exit the building. So they started having fire drills.

Lunch time at PS 36 was a nightmare. We begged our mother to let us come home for lunch. Students were only allowed to go home for lunch if their mother was home. I couldn't stand the cafeteria. One time, someone had put an open milk container on top of a girl's head and the milk was just dripping down her face and all she did was cry and no one came to help her.

My mother let us come home for lunch by ourselves. It was hard walking home in the cold and even harder to walk back to school. We did it because it was better than eating lunch at school.

The school had old classrooms, hallways, bathrooms; it was just an old building. It probably should have been torn down but, because of the baby boomers, they needed the school no matter its condition. It was eventually torn down, though.

The desk and seats were one unit and nailed to the floor in straight rows, all facing the teacher's desk and blackboard. There were no moving desks around. The blackboard or chalkboard had to be washed every day and the chalk would get all over everything. The erasers had to be cleaned outside because the chalk dust would choke one during the cleaning. Not very healthy for the lungs of children or adults but that's what they used in those days.

There was an easel in every classroom. That was our art class. I loved it when it was my turn to paint at the easel. I would watch the other kids paint instead of the teacher. I would paint on the large piece of paper on the easel and show my artistic talents. Usually a simple child's painting with the sun high in the corner and a house with windows and flowers in the window box. I wanted to live in a house, so I would paint houses often. Sometimes I would make figures. I wished I would have had drawing lessons and some crafty things to work with but the easel was what we had.

Gym was when the teacher decided to take the class to the empty cafeteria and play games. I remember dodge ball and pretending to be animals, such as elephants and walking around in a circle. There was no music instruction that I remember. There was the glee club I tried out for but didn't make it. My sister did. There was a big assembly for the glee club and my mother and I went, there were many kids. They sang nicely. Everything seemed to be done in that one classroom with the one teacher. She had full control over all the subjects. Sometimes we would do craft projects, mostly during the holidays.

Father's Day was always a sad time for me. When the class made cards or whatever for Father's Day, I didn't know who to give mine to. One thing that is good today, they let the kids make things for any male figure in their life. They don't say "we are making a Father's Day card". I did like Mother's Day. I liked making a card or planting a flower for my mother.

They said prayers in the public school then. We used to have a prayer read every assembly. You also said the words Christmas and Easter back then. We would greet each other with "Merry Christmas" and "Happy Easter" during those holidays, even in the public schools.

There would be an assembly every Wednesday morning. You had to wear a white blouse and a navy blue skirt. The boys would wear a white shirt and navy blue pants. If you talked, you were ejected from your class and you would sit in the back with the other misbehaved students. I loved my second-grade teacher and I was a quiet child in her class. Somehow, I talked during the assembly and was put out in the back by someone. I just cried and cried uncontrollably. My teacher came over and gave me a tissue, I kept that tissue for days.

After school all of the kids walked home. There were no school buses. Everyone lived within walking distance of the school. It was always a mob scene leaving the school. They had maybe one adult crossing guard. Later, the older students volunteered as crossing guards.

Mostly you were on your own in a mob all leaving at the same time. Some mothers would come and pick up their children. I would watch as the mothers got their children on rainy and snowy days. They would bring boots and umbrellas and things to help keep them warm and dry. On those days, I wished I had someone to pick me up and give me boots or a hat. I walked home in whatever coat or hat, or no hat, I wore going to school that morning.

There was a boy who sat behind me who I liked but he wasn't able to do the school work. I would turn around and try to help him but the teacher kept telling me to face front. He was taken out of the class and a few weeks later I saw him in the hall. He had hearing aids in his ears with wires hanging down into a small box. I felt scared and shocked. He waved at me and smiled as if he were happy and skipped away. I just stood there. I hope I smiled back at him but I just couldn't move. It was the first time I ever saw anyone with hearing aids.

I'm glad he got the help he needed. Most of the time, parents refuse to accept anything being wrong with their child. As a teacher, I've seen hyperactive kids who could be helped with medication but the parents refused to take the child to a doctor. The attitude is they will grow out of it or it runs in the family. Middle and upper-class parents work to perfect what they have in their child. If the child can be helped with medication, there is a good chance he will get that medication. If they can fix something in their child, the middle and upper class do it.

I had seen children with big heads because at that time they didn't have a cure for hydrocephalus. I also remember a man fainting and laying on the ground having some sort of convulsions. It was frightening to see. I guess it's still upsetting to see. There will always be these things.

I was put in third grade with an experienced teacher. She was very strict. I thought to myself, *I guess I'm going to really have to work this year*. There was a class right next to ours where my teacher would open the door to talk to the other teacher. I would see all the kids running around. We used to make fun of that class. Then, one day, my teacher called some kids' names. I was one of them. We were sent to that class where all the kids just ran around. That's what we did all year. That's what I did in third grade, ran around.

I was part of the baby boomers' generation. There were too many of us. There was a shortage of teachers, schools, everything. Some of the teachers really couldn't teach, especially in the lower-income areas. The experienced, good teachers had their choice of what schools they wanted to teach in and usually it wasn't in the low-income neighborhoods. It was hit or miss with what kind of teacher one had. Also, the classes were large and the teacher wasn't able to give all the individual help children needed in these areas.

One time, it was snowing really hard, one could hardly see. My friend Beverly and I were between two parked cars waiting to cross the street. I stepped into the street and Beverly pulled me back as a car came whizzing by me. I felt it with my hands but it didn't knock me down or anything and my hands didn't hurt. The man in the car got out and hugged me and asked if I was OK. I said I was. He gave me his name and phone number and left. I told my mother that night and she asked me if I was OK and I said yes. That was that. Nowadays it would have been a different story, probably a law suit.

Today a parent would have made a big deal about it. I would have been taken to the doctor; but I survived and no one took me to a doctor. My mother didn't even call the guy. Who knows, maybe we could have gotten some money but no one sued anyone back then. I was fine, if I was hurt it healed in a few days.

Chapter 6

Back then, we were the first children to grow up watching TV. It was a good learning tool. It exposed me to middle-class life. I watched *Howdy Doody, Ozzie and Harriet, Father Knows Best* and many more. They all had lessons and showed different ways of family life. Maybe I didn't come from a family with a mother and father but I was able to watch one on TV. This paved the way for middle-class ideas. I now knew what an intact family was.

I also was able to see how a middle-class home looked. At first, I thought *who lives like that?* No one I knew lived in a beautiful house and had a car; but slowly I started getting used to seeing the middle-class lifestyle on TV and in the movies. Television is a very important environmental learning tool, especially for lower-income children. Before TV, how would the lower class be exposed to middle-class lifestyles and family ideas?

My mother would take us to playgrounds. There was one I remember going to often. It was all concrete. If you fell you got a bloody, badly scraped knee. I remember there was a first aid station in a little building and they would take care of any injuries. When I fell, I remember crying and going to the first aid stations and trembling while they applied antiseptic and bandaged my knee. Thank God they did away with concrete parks. Who in their right mind designs a children's park in all concrete. Parks were dangerous places for children in those days.

I also remember I loved the swings and the sliding pond. My mother would make sandwiches and we would play then have sandwiches. We sometimes went with her friend who had two children around our age. She also took us to the beach but it was a long train ride and a very tiring trip. So we didn't go there often.

The Projects had a central area where children could play. It had a basketball court and the apartment buildings were all around the play area. There were sections of bushes. These sections were chained off by small iron posts with one swing chain to keep the kids out. What happened was the kids, including myself, would jump over the swinging chain and sometimes not jump high enough and get caught in the chain and fall to the ground. If you were lucky enough to fall when you were jumping into the bushes, you fell on the dirt, if you fell on the other side you fell on concrete. I got many scraped knees doing that.

We mostly played hopscotch or jump rope in front of our apartment building. The play area with the basketball courts was left to the big black boys who liked to play basketball.

My sister got bumps on her neck one summer and my mother took her to the doctor. We soon found out that mosquitoes were in the bedroom biting her and that's what was causing the bumps on her neck. It was a big deal to be taken to the doctor in those days.

We did get all the childhood diseases going around at that time, measles, mumps and chickenpox. My mother had to leave us alone and go to work. She worked in a factory—a sweatshop, really—sewing parts of sweaters together. She was paid by the number of sweaters she sewed, or piece work. If she didn't sew sweaters together she wasn't paid. She didn't get sick days.

When I had the mumps, I remember being on the couch wrapped in a blanket watching television and not feeling well. My mother would come home at lunchtime and feed me and see how I was. She was in a rush to get back to work but at least she was able to come home and take care of me. I remember the mumps being the most painful. The chickenpox left a few pox marks but they faded in time. Luckily the big one that was going around we never had; that was polio.

We did get our tonsils taken out. All the kids got them out at that time. It was a horrible experience. I remember a mob of kids. They put us all in this big room then they put diapers on us. The little boys watched as they put diapers on everyone. I had to be at least five because I was standing up and I wanted them to stop taking my clothes off and I didn't want a diaper. Then I remember waking up in a crib with a sore throat, not knowing where I was. My mother picked us up and we threw up in the taxi on the way home. I'm glad they don't take out children's tonsils anymore especially in a big mob, such as that. It was a dangerous way of doing it. I heard of children choking to death because no one was around to make sure they were doing well after the operation. Parents were not allowed in to see the children.

We very rarely took taxis. I remember one horrible, rainy night my mother told us to wait on the sidewalk while she got a taxi. The taxi stopped and all of a sudden this man tried to get the taxi from my mother. My mother called us over to the taxi and we quickly got in but what an ordeal it was—you had to fight to get a taxi. Maybe it would have been easier to take the train.

We were in second grade and it was time to make our first Holy Communion. I remember many kids receiving their first Holy Communion. The public school would let us out Wednesday afternoons so we could walk over to the Catholic school and get religious instruction for first Holy Communion. We sat two kids to one desk. I don't remember learning a whole lot but I guess I passed whatever you had to know to receive first Holy Communion. It was hard walking to the Catholic school, especially when it was cold on those Wednesday afternoons but we did it.

We were put in line according to size and we all practiced where to go and what to do for Holy Communion. I saw my sister in line and started to talk to her and she pointed behind me but I didn't catch what she was trying to tell me. Then a hand grabbed my hair and yanked me to my place and that shut my mouth. It was a nun controlling the line.

My mother and Aunt Kay made our communion dresses, they were lace and mine was the prettiest dress I ever had. My mother bought us the veil from the church as we all had to have the same veil. She gave us a permanent and our straight hair was now frizzy.

The day of the communion was a beautiful hot day there were crowds of people. After the ceremony they just let all the kids out onto the street to fend for themselves and meet up with their families. I found my sister but we couldn't find our mother. I saw the other little girls getting bouquets from their families and I said to myself *don't even want one, you know your mother can't afford that kind of thing*.

My sister and I looked around for our mother. We were starting to get worried when we saw her. She was holding two little white bouquets with one pink rose in the middle. Oh my God, I was never so happy. Until this day I remember how it felt to get that bouquet. We kept it in the refrigerator for days. I still can see it in my mind. It was the most beautiful thing I ever got. We didn't have a party or any kind of celebration but I didn't need one. I was so happy getting that bouquet.

We went to visit my Aunt Kay and Uncle Tommy to show them how we looked. My Aunt Kay was doing laundry with an old washing machine with a rolling apparatus to ring out the clothes. They congratulated us then we went to visit an old lady in a wheelchair. She gave us some money. I think it was the people for whom my mother did housework. We must have visited other people but that's all I remember.

We did get our picture taken and I have it somewhere or maybe my sister has it. I remember it and could tell you exactly how it looked. My first Holy Communion was one of the most special days of my childhood. Now I know it was the most special.

Chapter 7

There was a girl in my class who came to school in pretty dresses. I wanted pretty dresses but knew my mother couldn't afford them. We got three new dresses and a coat at the beginning of the year and that was what we wore.

Nowadays, most public schools have uniforms. They don't look to be uniforms, though. They have navy, beige, red and white shirts, pants and skirts. By the time the child uses all the combinations it doesn't look like uniforms. It's great for the poor kid. They get to look the same as everyone else. They don't have to see others wearing pretty dresses or have the other kids see they can't afford the expensive clothes.

Just as lower class families can't afford designer clothes, they also can't afford lessons. I wanted to take ballet lessons, because my friend had taken them. My mother said she couldn't afford ballet lessons for both of us so neither of us could go. There were many things she couldn't afford for both of us.

This is one of the main things middle class and upper class families have over the lower class families, the means to pay for lessons for their children. Getting private lessons builds up the child's self-esteem and their enthusiasm for creativity and ability to feel confident in their worth.

I just was so tired of not having anything. I was tired of not having expensive clothes and of not being able to afford ballet lessons or not being able to afford just about everything I wanted. I was fed up with not having a mother who could be home when I got home; of not having a mother who could pick me up after school when it was snowing or raining. I was worn down by not having a father to take care of me. I was just so tired of being poor.

One day after school, I just went to every unlocked classroom and looked for stuff I wanted. I didn't find much but one teacher's desk had red and blue colored pencils, so I took them. My sister told my mother I had those pencils and she wanted to know where I got them. My sister told her I stole them and I was scared. My mother told me not to do that anymore; so I never did, I was too scared of what would happen. I never used the pencils. I learned then, even if you don't have what everyone else has, or you want what you can't have, you can't steal to get it.

Memories

One time, when we went to buy shoes, my sister whispered something to my mother. My sister had asked for another pair of shoes, she told my mother she wore her shoes out faster than I did. I defended myself and said she didn't wear out her shoes faster than me and she had the same shoes I had. My mother then told my sister she couldn't have an extra pair of shoes.

We would go to the city camps for two weeks up in the Catskills during the summer. One year my sneakers had a hole in the sole but my mother didn't have time or money to buy me new ones before I went to camp. She said she would send me a new pair. When I was at camp I put cardboard in the sole to cover the hole but that would wear out fast. I asked the art teacher if she had any leather so I could put it in my shoe. She didn't. I remember trying to walk on grass so my foot wouldn't hurt so much. Finally, my sneakers came in the mail. I was never so happy to get shoes. I was so grateful my mother had sent them.

When I was at camp, everyone was singing, following along in the song book. I couldn't follow along because I didn't know how to read music. I thought you read it the same way as when you read a book. A nice lady came up next to me and just pointed to where I was supposed to read and sing and that's how I learned how to read a song.

My sister and I were in separate camps. They wouldn't put twins together. We were in separate classes, too. The first public camp we went to when we were very young let us go together. We didn't want to be at camp and we wrote a postcard to my mother and asked her to take us home. She didn't.

We didn't like it because the counselors made you eat your vegetables.

I remember resting and my leg was off the bed and a counselor telling me to put my leg back on the bed a few times. I couldn't understand why I couldn't keep my foot off the bed. Then, when rest time was over, I was tired.

They had a list by the bathroom and wanted you to check off when you went to the bathroom. I don't know why they needed that information but apparently they did. I remember peeing the bed. I hadn't done that in a long time and the counselor dragged the mattress out in the sun and had it dry the next day. When I went and told the counselor I peed the bed she said I could sleep with her. She didn't make a big deal out of me peeing the bed. I slept with my sister.

One time when my sister and I slept in the same bed over at my Aunt Kay and Uncle Tommy's house, we woke up and one of us had peed the bed. They put us both in a corner and embarrassed us by telling everyone what we had done. I didn't pee the bed, my sister had but we both were punished for it.

We went to free public camps separately for a few years. I really liked it and cried when I had to go home. I loved being in the country by a lake. I loved going to the mess hall, loved bug juice and having three scheduled meals a day. It was wonderful to pick what activities I wanted to do that day. I tried doing archery. I always made such wonderful new things in arts and crafts, which I brought home with pride. We swam in the lake every day. The little bit of swimming I can do is because of camp. I loved the freedom of being outside, picking and choosing what I wanted to do. I loved taps at night. I didn't want to go home. I would have stayed the whole summer if they would had let me but the public camp only allowed you two weeks.

When I came home from camp one time, my mother told me a little girl had been hurt very badly by a mean man right in front of our building and now she was in the hospital. My sister, who had come home from camp a few days before, saw the man getting the girl to go with him. My sister was in the group of children to whom the man was talking. She had run into the apartment and watched from the window how the little girl was talked into going with him. The next thing she heard was the little girl was in the hospital because she had been badly hurt. She felt as if she should have done something because she had a bad feeling about the man, which was why she ran into the apartment. She saved herself but she couldn't save the little girl.

My mother wanted me to get my sister over feeling bad. So we played a little and we talked a little and in a few days she seemed to be OK. I think she still remembers it and still feels as if she should have saved the little girl; but, really, what could she have done? She was a kid herself. Poor children are unattended and are at the mercy of things happening to them. If they don't learn to be cautious very quickly, they will probably be one of the unlucky ones.

Then, one year, my mother's best friend sent her daughter, Lucy, to the Catholic camp and raved about it. Even though it cost money my mother decided to send us. We got to the camp and saw Lucy. She seemed happy but we soon found out it was not the same as the free public camp.

First, the nun washed our hair with smelly shampoo because she said we had bugs. Then she put us in bunk beds. In the morning before breakfast, we were all lined up and marched to the outdoor chapel to pray. Then we went to breakfast and, afterward, we marched out to the chapel to pray again.

Arts and crafts consisted of sitting around waiting for the nuns to decide what they were going to do then giving us a jar to paste a holy picture on.

The days were damp and cold and my bathing suit was still wet from the day before. I didn't want to put the wet thing on to go swimming. The nun said I had to do it. In the public camp you were never forced to do anything. If you didn't want to go swimming they didn't make you. So I ran back to the bunkhouse and I looked out the window, thinking about how I could get away and go back home. I saw people getting into their car and thought maybe I could ask them to take me back to the city; then thought the better of it.

The nuns came and got me. At dinner that night a big, tall nun came and took me out of the dining hall. I was standing next to her when I saw them marching everyone out of the dining room and making a big semi-circle around me and the nun. I was scared; the nun took me over to a big pile of wood and told me to pick out a big stick. I shook my head no. She picked one for me then she held one of my hands and started hitting me on the behind with the stick. She said this is what happens when you try to run away.

Then it was over and they marched all the kids into the chapel to pray, including me. The next day a few of the girls would point at me and say, "She is the one". I put on my wet bathing suit the next day and I did go swimming and I never did try to run away again but I hated the camp and couldn't wait to go home.

When the two weeks were up and my mother came to pick us up, I told her what the nuns had done. She said she would never send us back there and we would always go to the free public camp from now on. She said, "What do you want me to do, fight the nuns?"

Well if we had been middle class she would have. She would have had the money and the expertise to do something about what they did; but, in those days, people in my class just took it. We were used to nuns, brothers, and others beating us. We would beat each other. Family members beat each other. That's what we knew, that's what we did. We were used to it.

Even at that time, I knew there had to be a better way. I saw the better way in the public camp. They didn't hit the campers. They were thoughtful and kind and wanted us to have fun, not conform, pray and obey. Middle-class attitude isn't one of beating someone to get them to do what you want. Middle-class attitude is more gentle and kind.

We got older and we had to go to junior high school. The junior high school in Williamsburg,

Brooklyn had a really bad reputation so my mother's friend, whose children were in the Catholic school, told her to try to get us into the Catholic school. My mother was able to get us in but they put us in 6th grade instead of 7th grade. That was the grade our birthday said we should be in.

My mother putting us into kindergarten a year earlier than when we should have started school finally caught up to us. At the time, she needed us to be in school so she could work but now the Catholic school wanted us in the right grade for our age.

We were embarrassed when Cookie and Judy found out we were put back a grade. We felt as if we had been left back. It didn't do us any good being in the right grade starting in 6th grade. The damage was done. We had missed getting the fundamentals at the right age.

There were big classes in the Catholic school. Our class had fifty kids. My sister and I were in the same class. We wore uniforms. The nun didn't like my sister's hair so she combed it for her. My sister wanted to leave the school. She was so humiliated and angry.

Lucy tried to be nice but she would say things, such as why don't you know the prayers by heart, I knew them the second day I was here. I learned the Hail Mary, Our Father, and a few other prayers by heart. I learned to become very narrow religious minded.

They taught everything according to the religious way. Don't wear makeup, don't do anything with boys and don't wear revealing dresses, no high heels. Catholicism was the true religion, only marry a

Catholic, have many children, no birth control, don't eat meat on Friday, live by the Ten Commandments. No divorces, I was afraid they would find out my mother was divorced. No abortions. Be kind to everyone, never boast, never be bossy and always be meek. Go to church on Sunday or it is a mortal sin and you will go to hell.

It was a very narrow way of relating to life and not one you really could use in the real world. You almost had to unlearn what they taught you to survive in the real world. It was almost a way of keeping the lower class in its place. Women, especially, were taught to be submissive, meek and naive.

One time, I saw a nun throw everything off her desk because some of the kids forgot to put their number on the upper right-hand corner of their test paper. She had a tantrum over that. She put a boy under her desk because he was misbehaving. She also put him in the closet.

After one of the assemblies, the whole school was in the hallway and it was a crowd of students. The nuns wanted to get control of us. We were making too much noise. The head nun beat up a girl so bad to make everyone stop talking; we all shut up and marched into our classrooms in silence.

We just stood there in horror and heard the girl screaming so we all went quiet really quick. I saw the girl when I was going into my classroom, she looked as if she had just been brutally beaten, her face was red from the punching and she looked to be in pain. It was amazing what the nuns could get away with back then.

Chapter 8

My mother didn't go out with many men. I can remember only three in maybe ten years. She went out with a Jim, who I remember as being very quiet and not very friendly. I think he was a cop. Then there was Enzo, who I liked because he brought us pastries and he was friendly. My mother almost married him but when she called his ex-wife, she found out he had a drinking problem. I guess she had an idea about it anyway.

She decided to marry my stepfather or she was grateful to marry him. She acted more as if she were grateful he married her. I remember after they were married, my stepfather calling us in the living room. He showed us one of our dolls on a chair with her behind up in the air and said that is the way your mother wanted to marry me. He was a very crude man.

My mother had low self-esteem. She didn't think she was a good catch; she felt she had to be grateful that any man married her. She was hardworking and willing to cater to a man. Any man should have been grateful and thankful to get such a woman but no, she gravitated to men who felt they had the right to be treated as if they were the master and she was their property. She was actually a good catch except for having two children. My stepfather didn't keep her in the lap of luxury; she still had to go to work. Now she catered to him and whatever he wanted and needed, she did.

That kind of relationship is doomed for unhappiness. Most lower-class women stay in such relationships. They are treated like doormats and property and they stay because they can't financially take care of themselves or their children. They even stay when they would probably be better off by themselves. They were brought up to believe they needed a man.

My sister hated him. She didn't want them to get married. I thought it was fine. My mother's best friend was the maid of honor. She wore a beautiful glittery dress and my mother wore a blue suit. The maid of honor shined more than the bride.

We went with them on their honeymoon to Florida. It was the first time I ever went anywhere. On the long drive there, we stayed in houses that rented rooms. One house was scary as a haunted house. The people who lived there looked as if they were out of a horror movie too.

Memories

My mother and stepfather had a fight when we got to Florida because they couldn't find some relative of my stepfather's with whom we were supposed to stay. They eventually found them and we stayed in a little bungalow. It was beautiful, with palm trees, coconuts, warm weather. We even went to school there. It was a new, beautiful school with outdoor hallways, and everyone was quiet and nice. The classrooms weren't air-conditioned but you really didn't need it, it was winter. I just loved the school.

When we got back to New York my stepfather moved into our apartment in the Projects. He was an ignorant man with no manners or class. His idea of playing with us was to lie on the bed and try to put his feet in our mouths while we tried to put our feet in his mouth. I really didn't want to play that way but I thought that is what my parents wanted me to do so I did. We did that a couple of times and then my mother asked us if we wanted to do that and we said no. So luckily, that stopped.

When my mother made muffins he would touch every muffin before anyone was allowed to take one. So if you wanted one you had to take one he had touched. At least I can say he didn't have a drinking problem, or a gambling problem, he did go to work every day, he did have a car and I did like being driven around. My mother did seem happier. She had someone with whom to share life.

He did have personality faults, though. This was his third marriage. He was a very nervous man and everything was a big deal to him. When our new

TV was delivered, my stepfather was so nervous he could hardly control himself. We were told to go up to Cookie and Judy's apartment and we looked at the TV from their window when the men were carrying it in. He was a very ignorant, stupid, unworldly man. Nonetheless, we all seemed to kind of get along but it was uncomfortable.

I didn't feel as if I was accepted or wanted. It was as if they had to keep us with them. He rarely acknowledged us; he mostly ignored us or told my mother what she should tell us to do. There certainly was no love between us. I wanted to be seen as little as possible. So I tried to avoid them, as much as possible.

We soon moved out of the Project to a small house in Forest Hills. His family had found us the house. I found out years later that my mother's friend's children were jealous of us moving to a house. I was happy to move to the house. I had never lived in a house. It was a nice experience. I got my own room. My sister got the bigger room and I got the smaller middle room. I painted my room blue and decorated it to my taste and I loved it.

The house had railroad rooms on the bottom floor and three bedrooms and a bathroom upstairs. You walked in the front door to an all window porch and then into the living room, dining room, with the stairs up to the second floor, the kitchen was in the back. It had a back door and a detached garage and a little back yard. There were rose bushes by the steps going down to the back yard.

I remember my mother said the moving men were impressed that we were moving to a house and out of the Projects. My stepfather was a nervous wreck when we moved. We all had to be so careful what we did or said when we were around him. Everything got him upset.

He was taking a box from the basement up to the kitchen and he hit something and threw the box down the stairs. He supposedly couldn't do anything because he had a bad heart. If you went food shopping with him he would carry the grocery bag a block away from the supermarket and then give you the bag with which to walk the rest of the way home. I don't know if he really couldn't carry the bag or he just wanted to look good going out of the store then after giving me the bag so I could do the carrying. Who knows?

He really didn't do anything around the house. My mother went to work then cooked and cleaned. We did help with the cleaning. He came home from work, expecting his dinner, which he got then watched TV. This is the way it was. The woman was expected to do all the housework and cooking, even if she went out to work.

This attitude of keeping women down was such an unequal way of living. It was hard for the woman to live up to doing everything. Then, when she failed or became overwhelmed, she was accused of not being capable. So her self-esteem was beaten down. Here she was doing more than her share but treated as if she weren't good enough.

My mother had a painter come to give an estimate on how much it would be to paint the house. She walked around the house with him and he asked her what she wanted and she would answer just as a real rich lady. In the end, they couldn't afford the painter and she painted the house with our help. Our stepfather did nothing.

We would come home from school and my mother would give us each a wall off which to scrape the wallpaper. Then, when it was ready, we would paint it. My mother did most of the work when she was home from work in the winter. Soon the rooms were all nice, clean beige and all the old wallpaper was gone.

My mother and my stepfather fought a lot. He said he would never have bought the house if it wasn't for me and my sister. They were also having money problems. Some of their friends came over and told them they didn't buy the house just for the kids they were enjoying it too.

I remember when we were still in the Projects, my stepfather saying he didn't like the way the people looked at him and he wanted to move. At the time, I felt guilty for having them move out of the Projects. It's odd how a kid will believe what adults say and feel guilty.

That first year in the house they didn't have much money and my mother couldn't buy us new coats. My sister was upset and wore a sweater to school instead of her old coat. They bought us rubber soles to glue onto our worn out soles so the shoes would last longer.

We still continued to travel into Brooklyn to the Catholic school, which meant a bus, train and a long walk to the school. My arm felt as if it were falling off after carrying my school bag.

Memories

My stepfather's two nieces lived a block away and they had found the house for us. One niece had a girl our age but I never did get friendly with her. She was always on a diet and really into the way she looked. I didn't think she was pretty; she had her father's boxy figure.

She invited us up to her apartment. They had a dog and they dressed him up and made him dance. It was the funniest thing. They were the first to have an artificial Christmas tree. It was white. I thought it looked strange but beautiful. The niece would buy TV dinners then take the food out of the trays and put it on a plate so her husband really never knew he was eating a TV dinner. She had a big freezer where she kept them.

The other niece had two boys, one was about our age and one was older than us. They lived in a house right down the block from us. Her husband was nice but, when I first met him I didn't realize he was talking to me because he was cross-eyed. I kept turning to look where I thought he was looking. This may have annoyed him because he was looking at me. I think he worked for an airline.

The older boy would kind of be in the same group of kids we were. He was older so he really didn't hang out with our group. We would see him at the local ice cream parlor. One time, his group of boys came in and they had on sunglasses. When he took his off he had a black eye, some of the other boys did too.

The other boy used to hang out with us, sometimes. I remember we were playing ball and I threw the ball further than him. I went to my mother and said in a proud voice, I threw the ball further than him. Her reply was, "What is so great about beating a boy, who is going to marry you if you go around trying to beat a boy. So I went back and threw the ball again and this time I made sure I didn't throw it further than him. I went back and told my mother he beat me throwing the ball.

This was the train of thought for women back then, especially Italian women. The man was the boss. The woman obeyed the husband. The woman's career or ideas or wants didn't matter. The husband knew best and the wife did as the husband wanted. This is how I was brought up.

One of the nieces came over and asked my mother, "Why are your daughters traveling back to Brooklyn to a Catholic school when one of the best junior high schools is right here in Forest Hills?" I could have kissed her. She convinced my mother to send us to Russell Sage Junior High School. I was so happy. Only one bus ride away.

Chapter 9

We were put into the middle group of seventh grade classes in Russell Sage Junior High School in Forest Hills. There were fourteen seventh grade classes. Many kids were in that school. We would have eight classes a day and the class would move to a new classroom for each new subject eight times a day. We would have eight different teachers.

I loved it, a ways away from the Catholic one class situation. In Russel Sage, one time I went to my sister's math class and she went to mine because the teacher had us both only at different times. The teacher caught on and told us not to do that again. He was a nice teacher, he lived right next door to the school and sometimes he was late.

We started to make friends and first we got in with some girls that smoked in the bathroom. We all got caught and I didn't like getting warned, I didn't even like smoking. So I didn't hang out with them very much. I did get a taste of middle to upper middle class kids at Russell Sage. Some kids' families had money. They lived in really big houses in the private area of Forest Hills. They came to school in designer clothes.

Then we met Diane. She lived right on my block; she introduced us to Mary Ann, Grace, Eileen and Patricia. It was great. There was another girl who lived right across the street from me, Peggie. There were six kids in her family and she went to Catholic school. She became one of my best friends, so did Diane and Mary Ann. They all had a little bit more money than us but not by much; mostly because they came from families where only the father worked. The mothers stayed home.

Mary Ann was a big baseball fan. I would go to Ladies day at Shae stadium with her and see the Mets. Ladies were free on ladies' day. It only cost the train ride to get there. We made posters for the Mets, we rooted for them and Mary Ann taught me the rules of baseball. Until this day, I love the Mets and baseball is the only game I understand. I still love going to baseball games, especially when the Mets are playing.

Then we met the boys in the group. There were a few of them, John, Link, Mike, Pete, and Dennis. We would go to the local church for religion instruction every Wednesday night. The boys would be there. They broke us up into small groups and we would all have an adult to lead the discussion. We would get to see each other and hang out after the discussions.

A doctor led my group. It was the first time I ever expressed my opinion about anything. The doctor actually came to my house when I was sick and gave me a shot of something. My mother said it was good that the doctor knew me from the group, that's why he came.

I started to like one or two of the boys. I started going out with a boy named John. He took me on my first date. I was so insecure I didn't know how to act. I remember he wanted to buy me something and I got so nervous I told him I really wasn't able to pick anything.

He was nice. We hung out with the group for a while, almost similar to going out. He gave me a ring that was the kind you could bend to fit your finger and one of the prongs broke after I bent it a couple of times. He also gave me a sweat shirt that had lint or something on the inside; I tried to get it off but couldn't and gave it back to him. He asked me what I had done to it. I said I didn't do anything to it. I kept thinking he is going to tell everyone I dirtied his sweatshirt and I broke his ring. I think he did too.

Then, in my thirteen-year-old mind, I decided to go out one morning when he was walking past my house and break up with him. At first he was happy to see me then I just broke up with him and left him on the sidewalk not knowing what to do. A few days later I felt I made a mistake but it was too late. I tried to tell him but he said it was for the best we broke up and that was that.

I vaguely recall going out with a boy named Jamie who gave me my first kiss. He also gave me a ring. Some girl, who lived in the apartment next to his, told me he had given her the ring first. She said he had gone into her room and took the ring back and then gave it to me. I said to her "He went into your bedroom and took the ring?"

She said "Yes". I didn't go out with him for very much longer, it just seemed too strange.

I then started to like a boy named Pete. He looked similar to Tony Perkins and I loved Tony Perkins. Too bad Pete didn't love me. I took a picture of Pete and put it in a cheap frame and looked at it. We would all hang out at the school yard where the boys would play stick ball.

I would try to talk to Pete and pretend I was his girlfriend but he really didn't want any of it. We went to the beach as a group and when we all started eating our sandwiches Pete came over to me and said can I have a sandwich. I told him I didn't have an extra do you want mine, so to my horror, he took my sandwich and left me with nothing. He didn't even say let's share it. I was hurt but I still seemed to like him even though he cared nothing for me and treated me as garbage.

There was Artie and Jimmy. I went steady with Artie whatever that meant in those days. Artie seemed to think he was strong and would forever be picking up large things, such as rocks, to show how strong he was.

Jimmy would pick up girls and swing them around in circles. He did that to me one time and I felt as if my head were going to smash into something. Jimmy worked at the local fish store delivering fish on his bike. I begged my mother to have fish delivered, one time. She did but it came at a terrible time.

I was at the fish store and someone called and said Jimmy had to go home right away. He had just gotten my mother's order to deliver. He started to give it to me in his haste but I said I didn't have the money to pay for it. So he jumped on his bike and rode as a maniac to my house and delivered the fish. Then quickly rode home. I didn't do him a favor by having my mother order fish to be delivered. In fact, it was very bad timing. I don't know why he had to go home so urgently but he did.

Jimmy's mother and father had a membership in a pool club by the beach and they invited me and my sister to go with them. Jimmy had a sister named Joyce who was just about our age. We had to all change in the little cabinet so we all took turns. Once I left my bra out by accident and his sister accused me of doing it deliberately so Jimmy would see it. I honestly forgot to put it away.

Jimmy also stuttered when he talked and his mother would point her finger at him and tell him to take a deep breath when he was stuttering. I didn't like his mother; she was bossy. Jimmy had invited me to go somewhere and I didn't want to go and his mother got on the phone and tried to persuade me. I still didn't go.

He would have parties down in his basement. My mother made me a beautiful blue dress with an empire waist for one of the parties. I remember her friend was over when she was fitting the dress on me and she kept saying the waist is too high. Empire waist was the style in those days, that's what I wanted.

At the parties we would take turns going into the utility room with a boy. I went in with Jimmy during a few of the parties and we kissed but the last party when we went in he didn't want to kiss. My relationship soon cooled with Jimmy.

We once had a Halloween party down in our basement. All the kids in the neighborhood came. I dressed up as a devil because when we went to the local candy store they had horns and a devil spear, which I could afford. I put on red shorts and a black top and I was a devil. The boys came in all sorts of costumes; one boy came as a woman. It was really funny. Years later, someone said the boy who dresses as a woman at Halloween parties might be a transvestite. At the time I just thought it was funny. I wonder if that's true, I wonder if that guy turned out to be a transvestite.

I was so grateful to my mother for giving us the party. We had helped her clean the basement and get it ready for the party. She had made food for the party too. It was a wonderful party. I really felt as if we were starting to fit in with the middle-class friends.

Chapter 10

For a brief time, there was a boy who lived in the house next door. One night he came out when we were all on the street corner just hanging out. I said I never knew there was a boy living next door and he just shrugged. He was nice and seemed to really want to be friendly. He seemed friendlier with the girls than the boys. We soon learned he was a foster child who our next door neighbors had taken in. When the World Fair started, they took him out of his room and put a cot in the living room for him. Then they rented his room to people who wanted to go to the fair. I remember he showed us the cot and he said they are supposed to give me my own room. I felt sorry for him, especially because he was so nice. When he graduated from high school he went into the service, later he wrote us saying he had gotten married. I hoped he was happy. He deserved it.

I didn't like our next door neighbors not only for the way they had treated him but for other things too. When we first moved to the house, my stepfather only wanted us coming in the back door; he didn't want us to use the front door. That meant going down the long driveway to the back door. If we came home another way, we went around the corner then down the driveway to the back door.

Because we were the second house from the corner, our small backyard was right next to our neighbor on the corner and they had an open entrance leading into their backyard. We could get to the backdoor to our house from their backyard, a short cut.

This saved us walking around the corner down the driveway to our back door and in the cold, rain or snow this was a great short cut. You didn't have to walk on their grass or disturb any of their bushes or anything. They told my parents they didn't want us to use it, though. So between my stepfather only wanting us to use the back door and the neighbors not wanting us to use their back yard it was a hassle trying to get into the house.

I don't know why our stepfather wanted us to use the back door. If it was because our shoes were dirty, there was a front porch we had to go into first then the living room. It wasn't as if we had wall to wall carpeting. We had wood floors. It was just an old fashion lower class idea that he put on us to do.

In the end, none of them were home when we came home from school so we used the front door.

Memories

We only had to use the back door when my stepfather was home. After a while we used the front door more often than not. We always left the house by the front door. When it got cold and there was snow down the long driveway we used the front door. At least my stepfather agreed we didn't have to walk down the long snow covered driveway to the back door. I'm surprised he didn't have us shovel it. Thank goodness for small favors.

The neighbor on the other side of us was an elderly widow lady. She would sit on a folding chair in front of her house in nice weather and talk to everyone who walked by. Some people crossed the street to avoid her. My sister, Diane and I started to talk to her a lot. She would take us into her house and show us all the novelty things she had and tell us the story about it. Some things she got when she was on a vacation with her husband, some were for her birthday. She would tell us about her past. We would play cards with her and sometimes she would give us one of the novelty things. Usually she would want them back for some reason. One time, she gave us a bottle opening that had fur on it and the next day she asked for it back because she said it was sharp and she didn't want to give us anything sharp, it hurt friendships.

Diane got a little annoyed with her as did my sister and I. One day, we decided to tell her off about it. We were all outside her house and she was sitting in her lawn chair. She got very upset we should talk to her that way and asked a passing neighbor to help her in her house because she was so upset. She called my parents and told them we had been very rude to her. We were told to leave her alone and that ended our friendship with her.

My mother and stepfather would go on day trips. At first, they would bring us. We would go to a park with many geese and my mother and stepfather had folding chairs they would sit on. They brought nothing for us to sit on. We had to try to find some grass that didn't have geese poop on it so we could sit down. It wasn't pleasant.

It seemed they would let us come but have no accommodations for us, so we started to stay home. We would have to fend for ourselves at home because they would never leave us prepared food. We had to make whatever was there.

My stepfather didn't seem to want to have anything to do with us. Any time he did something for us, he got annoyed and aggravated. So, we almost never asked him to do anything. We just lived avoiding each other as much as possible.

One time, we had walked to the movie theater, which was about a mile away and when the movie was over, we got out and it was pouring rain. We were with Grace and she called her parents. They came and got her with their car. She asked if they could take us home but the mother said they didn't have room for the two of us and we should call our parents. We went to a candy store with a pay phone and asked the owner for a dime so we could call home and we called home. My mother didn't drive so my stepfather had to come and get us. When our stepfather came, he gave the man back his dime and drove us home. He was so mad at us. He had a big fight with my mother and told her he didn't want to have to do this anymore. I felt as if I should have just walked home in the rain, it would have been better than having this big scene. My mother said from now on we would have to have bus money so we could get home by ourselves but they still never gave us bus money. We still went everywhere with nothing in our pockets, most of the time.

I remember at the World's Fair, I was with my aunt and some other relatives and when it was time to leave she asked me if I had money to get home and I said, "No, I'll walk". She gave me money to get home. I still walked.

When we started going to Bishop Molloy High school dances the fathers of the girls took turns driving there and picking us up from the dance. I know my stepfather was the last to take his turn. I guess I should be grateful he actually drove us once but I was so worried and scared of what was going to happen after he drove us I couldn't be happy going to the dance. I was afraid there was going to be a big fight about it.

I loved Molloy dances. There were many boys around. The brothers would walk around and tell couples to get apart if you were dancing too close. It was the first dance I ever went to. We met a few boys and we went roller skating with them as a group. It was a lovely, exciting time.

Usually, we hung out with the kids in the neighborhood and went to the local ice cream parlor often. A boy we knew was a waiter there. Once Diane, my sister and I went there to have some ice cream. I usually got a hot fudge Sundae with mint chip ice cream. The boy came over to take our order and there was change on the table left by the previous people for his tip. He asked, "Is this your money?"

Until this day I don't know why but I said yes and took the money. Of course Diane and my sister knew it wasn't mine and looked at me with disgust. Then I ordered a banana split, I'd never had one. I regretted doing it, immediately. When we finished and went home my sister told my mother. She didn't say anything. I wanted to go back and give him back the money but I didn't have any money to give him, so I just went up to my room. After that, the word got out about what I had done and no one wanted to be around me anymore. Luckily, we were just about to go to high school.

Chapter 11

Junior high graduation was on a beautiful summer day. The graduation was held in a movie theater and we were all standing outside greeting each other. I had on a blue shirt with a flower top that I had sewn. We had started to make our own clothes.

One boy came up to me and said why aren't you dressed for graduation. I told him I was dressed for graduation. He walked away then came back a few minutes later and told me I looked very nice but I knew I didn't look very nice. I was totally underdressed; he was just trying to make me feel better. I didn't feel better.

After the graduation, my mother said let's go to the store so I can buy you a graduation dress. We went to the store and I tried on a few dresses then my mother said it makes no sense to buy you a graduation dress now graduation is over and we went home. She was right it made no sense to buy a dress now I had missed the moment. I should have thought about a dress before graduation. I guess I thought the blouse and skirt I made was good enough. It wasn't in that middle-class atmosphere. I started to learn to be middle class. You had to dress the part.

To my mother's astonishment, we wanted to go to Art and Design High school in Manhattan and not Forest Hill High. Even more to her astonishment was we both passed the drawing test to get in. We started Art and Design High School.

I loved art, I loved drawing and painting for as long as I could remember. When I was about three I drew a big round circle on the wall with all my crayons. That may not have been drawing but I remember liking the colors. I also remember I drew it on the wall behind a chair so maybe I knew I wasn't supposed to do it.

In elementary school, I always wanted to go to the easel and paint. My mother had to tell the teacher not to let me go so often. I quickly started to copy fashion figures from the newspaper when I got older. I did that for a number of years. I would love to draw faces of people. When someone came over, I would ask them if I could draw them. After our first year in middle school, they put me in the art class. So I don't know why it came to a surprise that I wanted to go to Art and Design High School

Even though we had to take the bus to the train and then walk to school, I loved it. It was a very progressive school, the first thing I remember was a terrace you could go out on during lunch and smoke if you wanted to. I did that once but didn't like smoking so I never did it again. When it got cold there was no reason to go out on the terrace. There were escalators that you used to get to the different floors. It was a fairly modern building and it looked beautiful to me.

There were many different kinds of kids who went there, different from the ones I knew in Forest Hills. There were kids who came to school in limos, kids who lived all over the city, kids who were outwardly homosexual, poor kids, rich kids, nerds, there were not too many jocks but all of them were artists, were talented artists and serious about art. Some kids dropped out the first few weeks and went to their local high schools. Others loved the school and stayed. I loved the school and stayed, so did my sister.

We were exposed to all different classes of kids. It was a very heterogeneous group. We made friends with all types of kids—upper class, middle class, lower class, they were all there and we all had art in common.

We soon found a group we started hanging out with and did so until we graduated. There were two sisters Maureen and Joan, and the boys were Steven, Richard and Robert. Maureen, Joan, Richard and Robert lived in Queens as we did. Steven lived in Brooklyn. They all seemed to be in lower class status as I was. It seemed even if you were put in a heterogeneous group you found people with whom you had the most common background. We did hang out with this group the most but we were friendly with other kids who happened to be in another status in life.

During our first year, which was our sophomore year, in those days you went to junior high in the seventh, eighth and ninth grade. So your first year of high school was spent in Junior high. It didn't make any sense but that's the way it was. During my first year in high school President Kennedy was killed. The principal got on the loudspeaker and told us and sent everyone home. I remember taking the subway home wondering what was going to happen. It was a very confusing time. I remember watching the whole thing on TV. It was horrible to watch.

Then came the funeral. Kennedy's little baby son saluting. It was heart wrenching. Then Johnson took over and there were rumors he had something to do with the killing. There were rumors and unrest but the country continued and Johnson stayed president. It seemed the protesting and the unrest just continued after that. The shooting of Martin Luther King and Robert Kennedy then the protest started for and against the Vietnam War. There were sit-ins and unrest from then until I was in my late twenties. Campuses were in turmoil, always fighting for something. Then there were shootings at Kent state and it just went on and on. It was this way all of my high school years even when I went to college but my high school years were still happy years for me.

We had art classes for almost half the day. I learned so much about art and drawing which helped me throughout my life. It was a wonderful experience. We learned from art teachers who were the best in their field. I grew to love art even more. The rest of the day we had our usual high school courses. After school we would meet our group and head to a local restaurant where we would laugh and just have fun.

Chapter 12

My mother decided in that we were in high school, we were old enough to work. She would send us on any job interviews she found in the paper. I remember going on a job interview for a typist. I had just taken a short typing course in Junior High. I didn't know how to type but my mother wanted me to go anyway. They asked me to type a sample for them. It was a total mess. I was so embarrassed. Of course, I didn't get the job. This did nothing for my self-esteem. Don't make a kid go to an interview if they know they can't do the job. No one should go on an interview if they know they can't do the job.

My sister did land a job after school at Sack's 34th street working in the bridal department selling wedding and bridesmaid's dresses. She would go every day after school then come home late at night. She gave my mother half her money and used the other half for transportation and food. One of our girlfriends sat down and did the math with her. By the time she gave half her money to our mother and paid for food and transportation she was left with five dollars exactly what she would be getting for her allowance. Plus, she was exhausted and she couldn't keep up her school work so she quit. My mother was furious and kept saying how selfish my sister was.

During the summer, one of my mother's friends got a job for one of us. So my sister took the job. It was office work and my sister worked during the summer. I stayed home alone all summer. I did go out with my friends when I could. One of my stepfather's nieces was a member of a country club and asked my parents if she could take me to the country club. I guess she felt sorry for me sitting in the house during the summer.

So my mother gave her the money for the guest fee and I went to the country club for the first time in my life. It was a beautiful summer day and we sat by the pool and had a wonderful lunch then went in the pool again. I know I didn't say much because I was afraid I would embarrass myself. I also felt as if I didn't belong and there was going to be some repercussion from going to the country club. I had a really nice day and was grateful the niece thought to bring me but I really can't say I wanted to go again. I was really afraid to go back.

Memories

A person gets comfortable in whatever class they are in. They get used to their situation in life. I enjoyed going to the country club but I was afraid of being there. It was very new to me, something I had never experienced. I was unsure of myself so I was a little uncomfortable. Then there was also, for me, the situation where I would be punished for doing something out of the lower-class parameters. The good part was I had been exposed to it. I saw there was another way for someone to experience summer other than sitting in the house.

Middle class kids learn how to swim, water ski, ride horses, sail boats and a host of other summer activities. They had lake houses, summer houses where they went to and enjoyed what the summer fun was. I didn't get to do those things but at least now I knew they existed. The TV was also a place where I saw what middle class kids did during the summer.

Unfortunately, what happens when a lower-class kid starts to date middle class kids is that the lower-class kids can't do anything. That's what happened to me. When I dated middle class guys I couldn't do anything. If they asked me to go ice skating I went but I couldn't ice skate. I couldn't ski, swim, ride a horse, sail, or do any activities. I couldn't show my stuff as the middle class girls could. I fell short in middle class activities. This was a big disadvantage.

Even if I knew a middle class activity I was at a disadvantage because I couldn't afford to have private lessons. I took a tennis class in college. I liked tennis. I started trying to play middle class kids. I was at a big disadvantage. They had taken private lessons.

Even if I liked it and wanted to play I couldn't afford private lessons to get better.

In my old age I joined a croquet club. I really like playing. I saw many members take lessons. At first I resisted, my old lower-class ideas seeped in. Then I realized if I want to be taken seriously I had to take private lessons to get better. Private lessons did really help. Get the right instructor and you can really improve. This gets you more respect from the members of the club and gets you into the group. They start to admire you and are interested in your opinions and ideas. I had no better ability then before but I developed my ability through a tutor. The first impression can last a long time. It is also very hard to change a first impression. So I learned to make the right first impression. If that meant taking private croquet lessons than that's what I did. That's what a lower class kid has to learn to do. Get out of the lower class ideas and change your attitude into middle class.

The middle and upper class work with what they have. They pay for tutors. the best they can find, so they can maximize their potential and shine. Thus, showing how good they are and then being accepted and admired. They also believe in plastic surgery. If you have a big nose as soon as you are old enough you can get a nose job. Even simple things, such as having moles removed are done by the middle and upper class.

I had a mole on my nose I wanted it removed. I asked my mother when I was a teenager to have it removed. My mother said it was too small to remove. She never even brought me to a doctor. It was ugly. It was a mole on my nose where a witch would have one. I finally had it removed when I was in my thirties. I'm surprised I didn't have it removed when I was in my twenties. I guess I didn't have the money.

Middle and upper class also know who you marry can make or break your life. The first rule of a good life is who you marry. The fathers usually protect their daughters from any undesirables. Just the idea that a boy has to go to the girl's house and sit down and talk to the father would rule out the undesirables. Middle and upper-class girls usually married boys of whom their fathers approved.

Remember Grace Kelly, she wanted to marry a divorced man and her father put an end to that. She married a prince, instead.

Back to my summer as a lower-class girl; sure enough there were consequences for going to the country club. Anytime I wouldn't do what my mother wanted, she would say, "I gave you money to go to the country club, do you know how long I had to work for that money?" At that point, I wished I had never gone. It just was too much for which I had to be grateful. I just started to feel guilty. I felt I had to pay back in some way for going. There was no way I felt I could pay her back. Luckily, the summer was soon over and we went back to school

Art and Design would have school trips. The music teacher had his classes walk to Carnegie Hall to hear a free concert. It was wonderful. We had such a good time walking together then sitting and listening to the wonderful concert. It was the first concert I had ever been to at Carnegie Hall. It was just great. Education is another way the lower class gets exposed to middle and upper class ideas.

We also went to West Point. That's when the girls left the high school boys and went on their own to see if they could talk to West Point guys. I didn't get to talk to any West Point guys but it was a great trip.

After school, we went to the Russian embassy it was Steven's idea. They actually let us in. We asked the Russian man questions about Russia. He was very nice and answered our questions. He then said he wanted to ask us a question. He asked, "Why did America have private and public beaches?" He would see crowded public beaches and right next to it a private empty beach. I think Steve answered that one. It was an interesting visit especially that we were coming out of the cold war and Russia had a bad image in the US.

We also met each other in Manhattan when school was out. Steven was the social director always into doing something. He showed me and my sister how to roll up a newspaper to make it hard and carry it on the subway so if anyone bothered us we could hit them with it. We cut school and went to the St. Patrick's Day parade once but we were so cold we never did it again.

We would go shopping together. Steven was always into making something so he could sell and make money. We all carried our large black portfolios instead of school bags so everyone knew we were Art and Design kids. One time, when we were in a restaurant, the manager called the school because we were making too much noise. One of the teachers came and told us we were the image of Art and Design High school and we should always give a good impression. So, we left.

My friends from Art and Design would go to each other's houses. Joan and Maureen lived in a house in Astoria. You could take a bus right into Manhattan and be left off right under the 59th street bridge by the school. Their house was a two family house, each floor had the same style apartment. Their parent's lived on the bottom floor and they lived on the top floor.

It was almost as if they had their own apartment. We would go home with them and it was akin to going to their apartment. We were left alone most of the time. Maureen and Joan liked to rest. Joan, who happened to be very pretty, would always want to go home to rest after school

Robert lived in a Queens house with his parents. He had an older brother Gasper. Richard, who also lived in Queens with his parents, had a friend called Nick. When I was introduced to Nick we started going out. Nick was tall with curly hair and we went out for a long time.

Steven lived in a railroad room apartment in Brooklyn with his parents. When I met his mother I kind of thought she might be an alcoholic. She kept rambling on about how her husband took her to a wedding and she had a good time. We didn't hang out at Steven's apartment very much.

They would come over to my house too and we had a good time. Usually they would come over Saturday night when my parents were out. Steven started going out with Maureen, my sister started going out with Richard, Joan started going out with Gasper and I started going out with Nick. That's the way it was for a long time.

My mother didn't want us going out so much and would tell us we couldn't go. Most of the time we obeyed but as we got older we used to go out anyway. She was still hitting us as if we were babies. One time, she hit me with a metal magazine rack and got the top of my foot so that it swelled. I remember hobbling over to my girlfriend Peggie's house across the street and her mother putting ice on it for me. Peggie was saying I was an abused child and her mother said I wasn't a child and this was not considered abuse. I hobbled to school for a couple of days.

I don't think middle and upper class parents hit as much as lower class parents. It was ridiculous how my mother kept hitting us even into our teens. My sister didn't take the hitting and one day hit my mother back. My stepfather and mother took her to a counselor for wayward girls. When they got there the counselor asked them if my sister drank, smoked, took drugs, had sex with boys, was pregnant, had any social disease or stole money from them. They answered no. So I guess the counselor told them they just had a normal teenage girl. They came home with my sister but my stepfather still was upset with her. My mother finally told him my sister was a normal teenager and to leave her alone.

Memories

My mother's friend's daughter was going to Junior Achievement and told my mother we should go. I went but my sister didn't want to go. I would take a bus, two trains and then a long walk at night to Junior Achievement. They taught us business strategies and gave a foundation in sales.

We were to decide what project we were going to sell. It was interesting but I was too tired to keep traveling at night to go. When Junior Achievement was over, my mother's friend would pick up her daughter and drive her home. I took the two trains and the bus alone at night to get home. I was tired and couldn't take the traveling anymore.

One time, after Junior Achievement, my mother's friend picked up her daughter and I went home by myself. It took me a good hour and a half to get home. When I got home I found my mother's friend and her daughter at my house. I couldn't believe she didn't give me a ride home. She told me she didn't know she was coming to my house or she would have given me a ride. I just felt so hurt and disappointed I didn't know what to believe. I always felt she thought her daughter was better than me and I wasn't worthy of her daughter's friendship. I never trusted her after that.

Middle class parents support their children by making traveling to classes easy. They drive them there and drive them home. They make it easy for their child to continue going to Junior Achievement. My parents had a car. It sat in the garage while I took the bus and two trains to Junior Achievement. Then the lower class kid gets the name they never finish what they start. They need help finishing. If I had someone drive me there and pick me up, I would have continued going too.

My sister and I are twins born on December 28, 1947 so our birthday was combined with Christmas and we got a Christmas present that also was our birthday present. My mother tried once to give us a birthday party in January when we were children but it really didn't work out.

My mother decided to give us a sweet sixteen party at the beginning of December. We invited the friends from the neighborhood and the friends from high school. My mother also invited her friends. I remember my friends asking what kind of gifts we wanted and I said nothing, just come. My sister was really mad at me but I felt I didn't want presents but she did.

Maybe I was too embarrassed to receive anything. Also, at that point, every time I got something I felt I was going to have to pay the consequences for it. I didn't want to get anything for fear of what I would have to endure for taking it.

Lower class kids get used to not getting things. At least, I did. Getting things seemed awkward and foreign and made me feel uncomfortable. You have to be exposed to things when you are young. You can't expect to be able to accept something when you are older if you never accepted it as a child. If I had been given presents all my childhood for my birthday that's what I would have thought was the norm. Because I never got birthday presents as a child, I thought not getting presents was the norm.

Memories

The sixteen birthday party was a great party held down the basement. Some of my mother's friends bought us gifts. We also invited my cousins Sherry and Gala. This was the first time I saw my cousins drinking. Gala had a beer can in her hand and was drinking it. First, she wasn't eighteen and second a beer can; so unlady-like. My mother also invited Arleen and her brother John, who had Downs Syndrome. After the party, everyone wanted to know if he was a relative. It was the first real big birthday party I ever had and I think I enjoyed it. I just wasn't used to it.

It was the sixties and we were into protesting. There were many protests, marches and sit-ins. One year, the High School decided we couldn't have field day. All the kids were upset. So we all decided to protest. First we all stopped buying school lunches. This still wasn't enough to get field day back. So next, we decided we wouldn't leave the lunch room so when the next group of kids came in there would be no seats for them. There would be a mob. We went around and told all the kids at the tables to stay sitting when lunch ended. We all refused to get up after lunch.

I remember a teacher coming to our table and telling us to get up and we just ignored her. Finally, the head teacher got on the loudspeaker and said the next group of kids had a right to have lunch and we shouldn't stop them from eating. He was a teacher everyone liked so we got up and left. The next couple of lunch periods the principal walked around the lunch room. They did give us field day but they called it something else.

The Beatles were also a big thing in the sixties. When they came to New York, Peggie's, the girl who lived across the street, father drove us to the airport at two in the morning so we could see them deplaning.

There was a big crowd of people at the airport waiting to see the Beatles. They lined us all up on the observation deck and as soon as the Beatles got off the plane and walked down the steps the crowd pushed to the front. I felt as if I was going to be crushed and was scared but I did see the Beatles. I did come away with a better respect for being in a crowd. To this day, I'm careful into what crowd I go.

The Vietnam war was brewing and there were protest marches in the city for and against the war. At first, I marched for the war; then, a few years later, I marched against the war. The boys would sit by the radio and listen for their number to see if they had to be drafted. Peggie's brother was drafted. Some boys would discuss going to Canada. It was a very turbulent time and it just got worse as the years passed.

There was also the civil rights movement with Martin Luther King, Jr. He was for everyone and for peace; but, unfortunately, he was assassinated just as the two Kennedys had been. It was a very sad and controversial time in the country.

I also remember the German measles epidemic. I got it and was very tired and sick for about a week. It wasn't supposed to be dangerous to the average person. It would be bad if a pregnant woman got it. When my sister was working at Lexington School for the deaf a few years later she had many deaf children whose mothers had caught the German measles when they were pregnant with them. The deafness was a result.

Chapter 13

We were about to graduate from high school and we asked our mother and stepfather if we could go to college. I felt this couldn't be all the schooling I was going to get. I wanted more. They said they couldn't pay for it. My mother said a junior high school teacher told her we weren't college material. My stepfather said our husbands would pay for our college. So I knew if I wanted to go to college I would have to do it myself.

This is so typical of lower class attitudes. One of the most important ways of getting out of lower class is through education. Different nationalities knew this. I once had a college professor who told me the Jewish immigrants who came to this country educated their children. They knew it was the way to get their children out of poverty. He said it took the Italians and other nationalities a few more generations to realize education was the way out for their children. My parents didn't realize that yet. They were to set in the old ways and thought that was the way for me also. Luckily I didn't want that to be my way in life,

I was a finalist for a scholarship at Cooper Union. I remember we had all gone to take the art test to apply for the scholarship. I was the only one of my friends to be called back for a final interview and art test. I didn't get the scholarship but was invited to apply to Cooper Union. I didn't because I had no money. I didn't even think maybe they would have given me a package that included student loans, so I could have gone. I just didn't even apply because I had no money and didn't think there was any way I could pay for it.

I also was a finalist for a scholarship to Farmingdale College out in Long Island. I didn't get that but was also invited to apply but I didn't.

Soon it was graduation and prom time. I asked Nick, my sister asked Richard but for some reason Steve, Maureen and Joan didn't go. We sat at a table with kids we didn't quite know. I remember my mother buying us long prom dresses. I got an all-white one with daisies on the top and a few daisies falling down the long skirt. My sister bought a light green long gown.

The boys didn't come to pick us up. My mother drove us to the reception hall where we met them. My mother had learned to drive. I remember the neighbors coming out and saying how beautiful we looked and told us to have a nice time.

As soon as we got to the reception my sister and I realized we forgot our I.D. We were eighteen but we had nothing to prove it. The reception was as a wedding only with no bride. I remember one girl was dressed as if she were a baby, all in white with a bonnet on her head. One girl at our table had a low cut dress with her bust just about falling out. It was a great reception and we had our pictures taken. We had a good time.

Then my sister, Richard, me and Nick headed out to an after hour club. As soon as we were out the door, two guys came up to us and said they had a limo for us. The guys negotiated and realized they wanted too much money up front and didn't trust them to be waiting for us when we got out of the after hour place. We took a taxi.

We went to an after-hour place called The Living Room because Nick knew they wouldn't ask for ID. We listened to some music and had a few drinks. We then started to go to a place where the Righteous Brothers were performing and they wouldn't let us in. So, we went back to Richard's house and had a few drinks until morning. We took a taxi home.

About that time, I felt Nick was going to break up with me. Sure enough a little while later he broke up with me. I was devastated; I didn't eat for two days. It was my first real heartbreak.

Art and Design's graduation was held in a movie theater. I had bought a white coat dress with a feather collar for graduation. I found it on the discount rack in Macy's and bought it with my five-dollar allowance money. So I had a dress for graduation maybe not the style I really wanted but it looked good just as a graduation dress. We all met at the theater Maureen, Joan, Robert, Richard and Steven and we took a group picture. I don't have the picture but I remember it in my mind.

We did keep in contact for a long time after graduation. We went to Joan's wedding to Gasper, her mother sat in the back of the church; she didn't want them to get married. They soon had two children. Unfortunately, they both died very young; Joan from cancer and Gasper from complications of diabetes.

I kept in contact with Maureen who got married and then divorced. I would go out with her to clubs and for some time we became Buddhists. We would go to Buddhist events.

Steve once got me a job interview where he worked but I didn't get the job. The last time I saw him I went to a wedding with him. He had been desperately calling all his friends trying to get a date for a family wedding he had to go to. I said I would go with him on one condition he took me home. We were just friends. I was doing him a favor but I didn't want to travel home late at night by myself.

Sure enough, at the wedding, they wanted to see Steve's girlfriend and there I was. When the wedding was over he put me in a taxi, paid the driver and kissed me goodbye. That's the last time I ever saw him.

I met Robert for lunch once or twice after graduation but soon heard he had died of a mysterious disease. He was bi-sexual, so I guess it was AIDS. At the time, no one really knew what it was.

Richard was the only one in our group who kept up his career in art; we all seemed to go to other professions, except him. As the years rolled by it became harder and harder to keep in touch until finally I lost contact with them. Years later I did find Maureen, she told me Joan and Gasper had died.

Chapter 14

My sister and I had jobs lined up before we graduated from High School. The local paper had run an article on the local high school graduates looking for jobs. I got a job as a spotter for a photography company a block away from where I lived. My sister got a job at a rug company in Manhattan.

Jobs are an interesting subject. There are many trains of thought about jobs and what kind of job you should get. I'm going to key into two kinds. One type of job you get because you are following your passion, the other type of job you get for the money.

First, it's great if you have the opportunity to get a job you are passionate about and you don't need to worry about how well it pays or maybe it pays well enough for you to live on. Yes, if you are in that situation take a job you are passionate about. Because you don't have to worry about money, you can key in on just loving what you do. Hopefully, you will be happy. Then again, maybe you will have a boss who tells you what to do and crushes your creativity and you have to do things their way and not your way, sometimes also crushing your passion for the job.

The second type of job is the job you get for the money. I also want to put into this category, the only job you can get. If you are lucky enough to get offered a job where you make much money, that is good. Sometimes just being offered a job is the best you have. If you need money for rent, food and other necessities, you need money so you take the job. That is the main concern of yours when looking for a job.

Sometimes you have to take the first job that is offered because the rent is due or you need money for food. By taking the first job, you might miss better offerors if you could have held out but you couldn't because you needed money. Your passion job goes by the wayside if you are hungry and don't know how you are going to pay your rent.

So it is interesting why people take jobs and their philosophy about jobs. Of course, the ideal position is one you love and be paid enough for doing. I wish everyone could have the job of their dreams; but lower class people often take jobs for the money. That's what I did.

About this time, I was telling people, when they asked me about my biological father, he was dead. I found it easier to tell them he was dead than to tell them how my parents got a divorce and he left us. People took the death story in their stride and the divorce story they wanted to know more. They even started to judge me about how I was brought up without a father and the father leaving. They seemed to think I would have psychological problems because of it. I probably did but I didn't need to be judged for it. I just found it easier to tell people he was dead. I told them he died when I was very young and didn't really know him. Most left it at that.

I remember one guy who worked in the Montessori school that I worked in didn't show up for work one day. When he got back he told everyone his father died and he just couldn't call. I was somewhat friendly with him and wanted to know more of the details and how I could pay my respects. He finally told me he did have an absentee father, he just overslept and made up the story about his father dying. He said he faked his father's death at least once every job he had. That's one way to make the absent father work for you.

The bus drivers at the Montessori school were young guys. Some of the young teachers started going out with them. One teacher told me the guys were into getting illegal drugs. She had gone with them to a drug store to give a fake prescription to get drugs and almost was caught by the police. I started to stay away from them. I knew I probably could be influenced quickly by one of them. I also knew if I got into any trouble no one was going to help me get out of it. So I stayed away from them and stayed safe.

I remember my first day of work, when I got home, my mother had set the table and decorated it and made a nice dinner. I told her I wasn't hungry. I was aggravated I wouldn't be going to college and she expected my life to begin by working now. I was mad at not being able to do what I wanted. I now had to go to work and contribute money. That's what I had to do so that's what I did but I didn't like it.

As a spotter in the photograph company I would color in the white spots on the photos, draw the eyes open in any of the photos that the person's eyes were closed and just touch up the photos to make them look good. These were professional photos from weddings and big important parties. I was one of three spotters. There was an old man who was a Russian Jew who would give me oranges and listen to the war in Israel on the radio. Then there was a Spanish woman with two kids and a husband. We seemed to get along fine enough. I worked there for a few years. One time, the Spanish woman told us that money had been taken out of her pocket book. Neither the older man nor I knew anything about it.

My mother and stepfather had been fighting much of the time. They were talking about getting a divorce. I was upset about it, so I started to talk to the Spanish woman about my parents. I told her they were probably going to get divorced and how upset I was. Then she said to me, "And that is why you took the money out of my pocketbook." I was shocked. I had just wanted to talk to someone and get some sympathy. Instead I was accused of stealing.

Memories

I told her I didn't take the money out of her pocketbook. Then I realized by telling her my problems she thought I was telling her because I took her money. What did I expect from her? Work is no place to tell your problems to anyone. For a while she and the old man seemed to think I took the money. Somehow she stopped accusing me because I think one of her children confessed they took the money out of her pocketbook. She told the old man, while I was there, I didn't take the money. So I was glad for that but she never apologized to me.

The old man taught me how to do certain spotting techniques on a photo and after we spotted the photos we would put our initials on the package. Once the manager came up to me with a package and said you got a complaint about this package, do it over. I looked and saw it was not my initials on the package it was the old man's initials so he had to do them over. I don't know why the manager assumed it was me. I guess because I was the new young spotter.

When I started working there in June there were two or three other high school graduates and we would have a good time talking and hanging out. Then at the end of August, they left to go to college and I was the only one who stayed. I wanted to go to college also. I especially wanted to live in a dorm but that never happened.

I started going to the Fashion Institute of Technology at night. I came home with $45.00 dollars a week. I had saved twenty dollars a week over the summer and had enough money to pay for two courses. My mother and stepfather took twenty dollars a week for my room and board. I was left with five dollars the same amount as my allowance had been. Because I worked a block from the house, I didn't have any transportation or lunch for which I had to pay. So this was a great help. All I had to do was take the train and the bus into the city to class two nights a week. So I could afford that.

The lower class attitude was to take half of the salary for room and board. I really doubt the middle class or upper class took money from their children when they started working. My parents were running the house before I gave them money. They could have run the house without my money but that was the way of our class.

In those days, women wore only dresses or skirts. They were uncomfortable and cold if you had to travel by public transportation, especially at night. The sixties styles were a little better because panty hose came into vogue and the stockings were a little warmer. The square heels of the sixties were more comfortable than the high heels of the fifties but wearing a dress was cold in the winter. We started wearing pants under our skirts or dresses then removing them when we got to work.

Finally in the seventies women were allowed to wear pants to work and school. It was a big production on what type of pants you could wear. It had to be a pant suit. Not just pants with a vest. At least it was warmer and more reasonable. After a while, it got a lot more relaxed and women were wearing jeans to work and school. At first it looked funny to me. Then I thought *how wonderful. Finally, what really worked won over fashion.*

I loved going to FIT. I took two art courses at first two nights a week, usually on Monday and Wednesday. I met kids in the cafeteria before classes and we would talk and have a good time. I met a girl who lived in the dorm across the street and I was able to see how a dorm looked. Even though it was hard traveling there at night by bus and train and even harder coming home later at night, I continued going there for the next two years.

Then a boy I met told me I could get a free education if I started going to Queensborough community college. All I had to do was pay for two courses and if I got a grade of C or higher I would matriculate the next term and then I just had to pay the registration fee. Well this sounded good to me. I was getting tired of having half my salary go to tuition and the other half go to my mother.

So I registered at Queensboro and the next term I was getting a free education. Queensboro accepted all my credits from FIT so in a little while I graduated from Queensboro and received my Associate degree. Then I went on to Queens College where, after a few years, earned my BA.

My sister started Nassau community college then went to and graduated from Hofstra. She had to pay the whole way. I remember her saying when the freebees for underprivileged students came; she never seemed to get there in time to get them. They were always given out by the time she got there.

She also told me she had taken out a low interest student loan and one boy had said his parents used his student loan to buy property and asked her for what did she use her student loan? She told him to pay her tuition. So the students in need weren't even getting the low interest student loans. The middle class students were getting them instead—those didn't need them.

I left my job at the photo place mostly because they moved. For some reason, my mother felt it wasn't a good job and would tell her friends my sister had a wonderful job in Manhattan and I had a low paying job in Queens.

I remember her friend said to me, your sister has such a wonderful job. What is the matter with you? Why are you in such a low paying job? I was shocked. I had no idea my mother was telling this to her friends. I had been perfectly happy with the job. Yes, it paid less than my sister's job but it was a block away from my house. I didn't have to pay for transportation, lunch or get up early and commute to work. Also I was able to have dinner at home before I left for school.

I told my mother if she really didn't like my job, that was fine but could she not tell everyone. At least just tell them what I was doing and let them draw their own conclusions. She told me she didn't like my job but she would try not to tell everyone my sister's job was better. The damage was already done, though.

I wonder if the lower class just doesn't brag about their children and the middle and upper classes do. It seems to me there would be more positive attitudes about their children in middle and upper class.

Chapter 15

My mother was never one to say positive things. She would mostly tell her friends negative things about us. She told our family and friends that I would drop all my courses at college. They were quite surprised when they found I had graduated. I remember my uncle saying to me "Your mother told me you dropped the courses you took and never finished".

I told him, "Maybe I dropped one course but I did finish and got my BA."

When I graduated there was no graduation party or any acknowledgment of the occasion. The only thing my mother wanted was a graduation picture. So I went to the studio and took a graduation picture in a cap and gown, bought one 8" x 10" and gave her the picture.

I didn't go to the graduation. I graduated in August, after summer school. August graduates weren't included in that June graduation. I had to wait until the following June and attend that graduation. By the time the next year came around, I had no desire to go to a graduation. Just about a year had gone by, feelings for graduation were over. I think now they let the students who are going to graduate in August attend the June graduation.

I was very grateful I was able to get a free education. On the whole, I learned a lot. At least it gave me an insight into middle class ideas. I may not have exercised them at the time but, at least, I became aware of the difference in attitudes. Hopefully, as years went by I was able to put some of them to use. It did give me a better chance in life.

I had a BA and a chance at more jobs. I think I got out of poverty because of it. I had a few jobs in different fields but mostly I consider myself a teacher. I taught for over thirty years. Teaching isn't a high income job but it is a middle class living, especially for a woman in the 1960's and 1970's.

In those days', women who went to college were mostly going to be teachers or nurses. At that time, many specialty colleges didn't accept women. Stevens College, for instance, didn't accept women for engineering. If a woman wanted to be a lawyer or some other male dominated profession, she'd better have some male figure looking out for her. Women were not welcome or wanted in those fields. The first women who entered male colleges were treated horribly. Many of them left not because they couldn't do the work but because they were threatened by the male students. Some feared being physically hurt.

In my later years, I met a man who went to West Point during the early seventies when women were first accepted. He confessed they did horrible things to those first women students at West Point. The women's lib really started in the early 1970's when many of these colleges got money if they accepted women.

Queens College, even though it was free and it gave me a great opportunity to better myself wasn't an easy place to go to school, especially at night. First the parking was practically nonexistent on campus. That meant you had to park on the street and that was horrendous. You had to walk blocks and blocks after you finally found a parking spot. There were rapes and muggings on all the streets near the college. I finally started to park illegally near the college just because I'd rather pay a ticket then be raped or mugged.

I was actually very happy when I got a car because going to school at night on public transportation was even worse. It was more dangerous than walking to my car. Jerry Seinfeld went to Queens College and when asked what he remembered most about it, he said there was no place to park.

I learned to drive when I started Queensboro Community college. That was a very hard college to get to by public transportation. You had a very long walk to the bus stop which wasn't pleasant in the rain and snow then waiting outside for the bus. After I learned to drive, I first borrowed my mother's car. Then I bought my own car. Mostly second hand cars that would constantly break down but it was a car, nonetheless. I used to sit in my car and study when I lived with my mother. I didn't have my own room. I slept in the living room. There was no 'your own space' there to study.

Registration at Queensboro and Queen College was a mob scene every semester. You had to get there early and wait in long lines to get the courses you needed before they filled up. If they filled up, you had to beg the professor to let you in, reminding him someone usually drops the class anyway. Nobody was there to hold your hand and make sure you had a pleasant experience.

If you started to fail a course, you got very little attention. You had to figure it out yourself. Some of the classes were held in lecture halls where there might be a hundred students in the class. The professors had student teachers who marked your papers and tests. At least you were able to get into those classes. Actually, some of the best professors taught those classes and I learned much.

I remember going to the Queens College registrar's office when I was ready to graduate. This nasty clerk told me I was one credit short for graduation. I knew this couldn't be because I would count every credit I took very carefully. She said "Here is your file," practically throwing the file at me. "Add it up yourself." So I did and sure enough she had added wrong. I had enough credits to graduate. Do you think she apologized? No she did not but I was graduating and getting my BA so I didn't care, I was happy.

My sister didn't get any acknowledgement of her graduation either but I remember my mother had a house party for my sister and her new husband when they came to New York from Colorado. They had been married in Colorado after living with each other for a year. At the party, my mother was so happy and proud of my sister and made a big fuss over her, rightfully so. One of her friends said aloud, in front of me to my mother, you have another daughter, too.

Marriage was important to the lower class. People got married young. It wasn't unusual for women to get married at eighteen. My sister was in her mid-twenties and that was too old in my mother's eye. She felt we should have married our first boyfriends when we were about eighteen.

Anyway, life went on and a fashion illustrator was my second job. I got the job by putting an ad in the paper. It was a fashion company located in Manhattan in the Pennsylvania building. I was passionate about this job. It didn't pay much but it paid enough. So, I started to travel to Manhattan every day. Directly from work, I went to FIT for my classes two nights a week.

I had been hired by an older lady who owned the company. She hired me while the other illustrators were on vacation. I was supposed to meet them when they returned. I was shown dresses on a rack and then I drew them on figures. I enjoyed it because I was using my drawing ability.

What happened though was the other illustrators never came back. There were only two of them and they both quit right after their vacation. I felt something was going on but I stayed and they hired another girl to help with the illustration. We became friendly and had a good time. After work we would go to bars that had ladies' night, the drinks were free for ladies. I felt to be a real fashionable middle class girl in those days.

This is when I had my first experience with drinking. During one of these lady's nights I drank too much and got sick. I also remember getting drunk once and kissing some guy I wasn't even attracted to. I realized I liked everyone when I was drunk. I decided I better be careful not to drink too much. Until this day, I watch what I drink and how much. I never wanted to embarrass myself again by kissing someone just because I was drunk. I was never a drinker so not drinking or drinking very little was not an issue for me. I can honestly say I never had any more embarrassing situations because of drinking. I'm not saying I never embarrassed myself again. I'm just saying I couldn't blame it on drinking.

There was a big flu epidemic and the owner of the fashion agency hired a doctor to come to the office and give everyone flu shots. I paid five dollars to get the flu shot and then came down with a horrible case of the flu. I remember I couldn't lift my head off the pillow for a week. Going to the bathroom took all the energy I had. I don't remember ever being so sick. Until this day, I think that was the sickest I have ever been. My regular doctor said I was given the flu shot too late in the flu season. It should be given right before flu season not during flu season.

My sister had forgotten her key and I had to go down two flights of stairs to let her in. I thought I was going to die. She was yelling at me because I took so long to answer the door. I almost didn't make it to answer the door, at all.

In the years to come they discovered medicine that helped if you got the flu. You had to take it within forty-eight hours of getting the flu. When you took it you felt better the next day. I had the flu at least three times after that and took the medicine and felt better, it was magic.

I was a relatively healthy girl but I did get migraine headaches, got many colds and I had allergies but didn't know it at the time. The migraine headaches affected my life the most. They would get so bad I would throw up. They plagued me until I hit menopause. I also got some relief when I went to a chiropractor. Mostly when I got a migraine it stopped my life for a few hours. I also learn to do things in advance in case I got a migraine.

The cold New York winters didn't help and I remember always having a cough during the winter. In those days, you didn't go to the doctor unless you were dying. Every time I took a TB test for a job, I had to get a chest x-ray because it always came back positive but lucky the x-ray showed I was OK.

I took the subway often. In fact, every time I had to go somewhere I took the subway. I took them at night on the way home from night school. The subways and my childhood made me realize how I reacted in a dangerous situation. I was never one who would start a fight but if you started one with me I would fight back in some way. I wasn't passive. I was always a little afraid when traveling on the subway at night. Nothing horrible ever happened but I did encounter some incidents. One time, I was standing by a pole waiting for a train and a man came up to me and said "I have a gun and if you don't come with me I'm going to shoot you". Well I just moved around the pole to get away from him and luckily a train came in the opposite direction so I just quickly got on the train and left him looking at me on the platform. I don't know if he really had a gun. I never saw it but I knew I wasn't going to go with him. I'd rather get shot in a public place where I would probably get help.

There were incidents where I saw men snatch women pocketbooks or take someone's wrist watch. I learned where to stand and who to stand next too. Don't stand or sit by the doors. That's where they snatch your pocket book just as the doors are closing and run. Walk with a crowd of people. Wear your pocketbook under your arm under your coat.

I learned to tell a man very loudly to please move when they were rubbing against me on the pretense that it was a crowded train. This worked, everyone looked at him and he moved. Eventually they put police in the subways and I learned to sit in the car where the subway police were.

One time, I was on a train and a woman was standing next to me, looking at me. She finally asked me, "Are you healthy" I replied yes. She then continued "Do you have any children or husband"

I said, "No"

Then she said, "My daughter is about your age. She has two children and a husband and she is dying of cancer." I was really surprised at what she said. I didn't know how to reply or what to think. Was she saying I should be the one with cancer and not her daughter?

I think I just said, "Sorry." I moved away from her. Life isn't fair, I didn't think it was fair to me money wise but it wasn't fair to her daughter health wise. Which would anyone rather have?

Soon the owner of the fashion agency put one of her friends in charge of the illustration department. She couldn't draw so I don't know what she was doing there. The other illustrator would make fun of her and so did I. She would tell us to do things with our drawing that just didn't make sense.

The other girl quit and I was left alone with her. I wanted to quit too but I didn't for fear of my mother's wrath. I had a disagreement with her about one of my drawings and she told the boss I was difficult to work with and she fired me. That ended my career as a fashion illustrator. I learned one thing: don't fight with the boss's friend.

Next I had a job working for American Airlines where all the girls, including myself, would sit at desks all in rows similar to a classroom and the manager, a man, would sit in the back and watch us. First I started in the mail room then I graduated to a desk. They gave me tickets from other airlines to sort into piles and that's what I did all day. It was so boring I couldn't take it and left. My mother was so mad at me. She was so disappointed and upset. She said I still had to pay her the money each week. She did suggest I try teaching. At that point, they needed teachers. So I got an assistant teaching job at a Montessori school and that started my teaching career.

At one point, after I graduated from college, one friend of my mother's sons worked for the New York City Board of Education. He knew of some openings in his department. I went to the interview and got the job. Because he worked in that department, he knew how I was doing. My observation came back as excellent. Of course, everyone knew what I had received on my observation.

My mother told me originally her friend wasn't going to tell me about the job because she was afraid I wouldn't be able to do the job. Now that I received an excellent rating, they were happy they did. I told my mother that was because she never told her friends anything positive about me. She always told them the negative things. So they had a bad image of me. If my own mother doesn't say positive things about me then would people think positively of me? My mother was silent. Because I was so good at the job, the department hired my sister too.

I don't care what social class you're in, you have to say positive things about your children. If the parents don't say and think positively about their children why should anyone else. Maybe middle and upper class people have a more positive attitude about life in general, thus saying positive things about their children. So, the children have a positive attitude about themselves.

Chapter 16

When we were still living in Forest Hills, right after high school graduation, my sister and I started going out with steady boyfriends. My sister was going out with Scott; I remember my stepfather had him paint the back porch and my sister got so mad that my stepfather had used him that way.

I was going out with Kenny. He was nice enough and treated me well but I wasn't in love with him. Kenny would come and pick me up and take me to a movie or out with friends. He didn't have a car so we went by public transportation everywhere. He had enlisted in the Air Force before we met. So in a little while, he went away to basic training. I wrote to him and I sent him things. I was going to school at night and working during the day, so I started writing less and less. He complained that I didn't write to him enough. I realized I didn't love him. I didn't want to marry him so why was I writing to him. I wrote him a 'Dear John letter', breaking up with him. He called me and told me he loved me and asked me to marry him over the phone. Of course, I said no as nicely as possible. So neither my sister nor I married our steady boyfriends, to my mother and stepfather's disappointment.

We were still living in Forest Hills and my mother and stepfather were fighting almost every day. Sometimes it came to pushing and shoving each other. My sister and I would sometimes find ourselves involved in it. I guess this influenced my sister's decision to want to look up our father. She went to the welfare department to try to get his address. They knew where he was but said they would get in touch with him and if he wanted to contact her they would give him her information. Very surprisingly, he did respond and my sister talked with him. He was living in San Francisco. They made arrangements for her to go out to San Francisco to meet him.

I had no desire to see him or talk to him and stayed out of it. I told my sister if he asked about me, to tell him I couldn't come to San Francisco because I didn't have the money. When she got to San Francisco she called and told me our father would pay for my air fare to San Francisco if I wanted to come. I really didn't want to see him but I had never been to San Francisco and it would be a free trip. So I went.

Memories

He was a big, tall, heavy man with beautiful, almost lavender eyes. He had been very handsome in his youth and there were still remnants of that. He managed a small hotel with his present wife. They gave us a room in the hotel and we proceeded to get to know our father. He seemed pleasant enough. I do remember having a sincere talk asking him why he left. He said my mother had the police after him for not paying child support and alimony, so he had to leave. He complained that when he came back to New York for his father's funeral he was afraid he would be arrested. I asked him if he ever worried that maybe my sister and I wouldn't be taken care of. He said he always knew we would be taken care of because we had a good mother and grandmother. He didn't say he was sorry he left or he knew he did the wrong thing. Nothing.

Then my father asked me if I remembered the time he hit my mother and knocked her out. I said I didn't. He said I carried on so he thought it would have some psychological effect on me. I still didn't remember. In my mind I felt I probably didn't remember because it did affect me and it was something my subconscious didn't want me to remember. Then I realized my father hit my mother and knocked her out and is telling me about it. Does he think that was OK to do? What kind of person does that?

My mother had always told us our father wouldn't work and she had to work and take care of earning the money. When she had us, she couldn't do that anymore and that's when the trouble started. Well, she was right; I saw it with my own eyes. His wife ran the hotel, she did the work; he really didn't do anything.

We finished our visit with my father. I wished I had never seen him. It just brought back an old hurt. We stayed in contact for a few months and when he came to New York we went to visit some of his sisters and brothers. I found out I had many cousins. Some of the male ones were in Vietnam. It was interesting to see all the people who were in my family but they were strangers. When my father left there was no reason to keep in contact with them. Because they lived in my area, I wondered if I would accidentally meet a cousin at one of the discos and start going out with them. As far as I know, that never happened.

I was busy going to school and working, and didn't have any real interest in staying in touch with my father. He was a stranger to me. It almost felt as if I was betraying my mother by being in contact with him. It just brought back old hurts. My mother would say one thing happened and my father would tell it a different way. It just wasn't worth it to me. I don't think he would have been an asset in my life anyway. Too many years had gone by. Too many times wanting him to come back and he never did. I guess I just got used to him not being there and that's how I was comfortable. I don't know if it was the best or the worst way; it just was what it was.

Not having a father in any social class is a big loss. In middle class your father plays a big role in how your life will turn out. Not only do you get the money advantage of a father but you get the positive support of the middle and upper-class father. Just having his presence when a boy comes to pick you up is a big asset. There are infinite pluses to having a good father. I could go on for pages and still not cover all the advantages of having a father. You have opportunities you would never have without a father. Just having the love of a father can make or break your life.

With or without a father, my life went on. After going to San Francisco to meet my father I wanted to see other places. Peggie, the girl who lived across the street, invited me and my sister to go to Washington, D.C. with her and her family. I guess they had a station wagon because Peggie, my sister, Peggie's three little brothers, her parents and I all went to Washington, D.C. for a long weekend. We girls had our own hotel room and the parents and the little boys had theirs.

We went out to a club, and I was surprised to see MPs standing in the back looking at the crowd. The guys we met told us there were many military men in the area. The MPs were there to make sure the military guys didn't cause any trouble. Also, they stopped serving drinks at midnight. This was new. In New York you could drink all night. They also asked if there was really a big park in the middle of Manhattan and we confirmed there was, Central Park.

When we got home, we started planning our next trip and we decided on Boston. We were going up by bus and back by plane. I had met a guy during the summer who was going to Boston College and he invited me to come up and visit him. So we all thought this was a good reason to go because we knew someone in Boston who would show us around.

Well, my mother didn't like the Boston idea. She said we couldn't go. The only reason she let us go to Washington was Peggie's parents were going.

We were about twenty years old and making our own money, giving her half our salaries for room and board. We both felt we were old enough to make our own decisions. My mother continued to say we couldn't go and as far as she was concerned we weren't going.

The Boston weekend trip time came and we took our bags to work. We left straight for the bus after work. Peggie met us at the bus station. When we got to Boston we called our mother and told her the hotel where we were staying. My mother told us not to come home. We didn't think she meant it and proceeded to have a good weekend. I connected with the boy from Boston College and he took me to the college and showed me around the campus. I was very interested because I really wanted to see college life, dorms and things. After the trip, I kept in touch with him for a while and later he even came to New York and I saw him then.

We took the plane home. It was so exciting. The seats were not in rows, they were in a group facing each other so you could talk to one another. There were many seats in rows but we were put in the seats in a group. It was wonderful.

Peggie's father picked us up at the airport and left us at our door. They went into their house and we went into ours only to find my mother had packed our bags and told us to get out. There it was—the consequence of doing something I wanted to do.

Memories

We were too embarrassed to go to Peggie's family or ours, so my sister called a girl she worked with who lived in Brooklyn. She had a spare bedroom in her apartment. We both took the train into Brooklyn and stayed in the girl's spare room for about two weeks. After that we had found a furnished basement studio apartment we could afford so we moved in. We did have a phone put in and we called our mother to tell her where we were.

I did not like living with my sister. We did not agree on many things. I remember coming home from work and she had been home all day. She was mad I hadn't gone food shopping on the way home and brought something for dinner. I told her she had been home all day. Why didn't she go shopping and make something for dinner? We lived there for about two months.

My mother called us and said she wanted to see us. So we went to the house. She said she would let us come back and live in the house. We didn't talk about the conditions but I don't remember going on any more trips. We moved back and continued to give her half our salaries.

The fighting between my mother and stepfather escalated and they decided to get a divorce. They put the house up for sale. My stepfather stopped giving my mother money to run the house. She paid the bills with her money and the money we gave her. When the house was sold she got half, but nothing for the extra money she had put in. She was upset and said she shouldn't have paid the bills.

When the house was sold we had a few days to move out. One day, as soon as my stepfather left for work, my mother had a moving company move everything out. When my stepfather came home that night all he found was a bed, a little bit of food and his personal clothes. Exactly what the law said you had to leave someone.

According to my girlfriend, Peggie, he then went around to all the neighbors and showed them what the three of us had done to him. He showed all of my friends. I didn't go back there for years. I was so embarrassed. When I went out with Peggie, I met her wherever we were going.

I don't know if this kind of drama happens in all social classes but it seems the lower class is more prone to dramatics.

Chapter 17

We moved into a second floor apartment with a kitchen, living room, and one bedroom; and it had two attic rooms that my sister and I used as our bedrooms. They weren't legally part of the apartment because they were a fire trap, as they only had one way out. The landlord told us to get a rope ladder if we were using the rooms. My mother got us both ropes.

That first Christmas in the apartment was horrible. My mother decided to have everyone over to our new apartment for Christmas. I don't know why, there was hardly enough room for us, let alone a group of people. I remember the car broke down when my mother and grandmother went shopping. I remember everyone crowded around and some relatives sleeping over. I can't remember where they slept. I was glad when the holidays were over. It was a major adjustment moving out of the house.

My mother started looking for a house to buy with the money from the sale of the Forest Hills house. She bought a one family house that had been converted to a two family in Ozone Park. The first floor apartment had a kitchen, bedroom, and living room; the bathroom was down in the basement. The upstairs apartment had a kitchen, bedroom, living room, and bathroom. My sister and I begged our mother to let us rent the upstairs apartment, but she said no. So we all moved into the three rooms downstairs. She rented the upstairs apartment. We still gave her half our salaries for room and board even though neither of us had our own room.

At first, I said I would sleep in the basement. The basement was unfinished and had no heat. When it got cold, I came upstairs to sleep. We had two beds in the bedroom and a fold out couch in the living room. I slept on the fold out couch in the living room.

I was unhappy with my living conditions and wanted to go somewhere or do something. The only good thing about living with my mother was after giving her half my salary I had money left over to save.

I saw the movie *Rome Adventure* with Suzanne Pleshette and Troy Donahue and decided I wanted to go to Rome. So I started to save every extra penny to go to Rome. I wished I was the daughter of a middle-class Jewish or Italian family who sent their children to Europe for a vacation but I wasn't.

I certainly wasn't middle class, I didn't have the middle-class money; but I wanted to at least look and act like I was. I think the middle class is a state of mind and a state of money.

One Saturday morning I was with my sister and mother in the 1958 Chevy. I had $5.25, just enough for my expenses that week. My mother asked me for gas money. I was annoyed at this. I gave her money every week, why did I have to give her gas money too.

I told her I didn't have it. My mother didn't believe me. I told her I was on a tight budget because of my trip to Rome. She felt a couple of bucks wouldn't hurt my budget for my trip to Rome. I knew it would, I knew this was the turning point that was either going to make or break my saving enough to go to Rome. I didn't give her any money.

My mother looked me straight in the eye and there was a long moment of silence then she gave a little sigh and turned away and started the car. I was waiting for the consequences but there were none.

One year later, I had saved enough money to go to Rome. I had saved a thousand dollars and booked a plane ticket on Icelandic Airlines that landed in Iceland, then Luxembourg. From there I was taking a train to Rome. I would be staying at the Hotel Adriano where I would be rooming with other girls who would be taking courses at the Rome Institute. I didn't want to be totally alone in Rome so I had decided to go on an education group tour.

My mother didn't like the idea but she didn't do anything about it. I was over twenty-one at that point and I guess she had softened. I still gave her the money for the month I would be away.

I recall Monday, July 28, 1969 was the day I flew to Rome. I put all of my blouses, skirts, slacks, and underwear into my suitcase. It wasn't too heavy. Luckily I didn't have too many clothes. I brought the toilet paper my mother's friend told me to take. I really didn't need it.

I left from JFK. I would arrive in Iceland and stay the night. The next morning, I would fly on to Luxembourg, where I would stay a night and then continue by train to Roma, Roma, not Rome.

I remember looking at the clothes I had decided to wear, my faithful black mini-skirt and my favorite blue, short-sleeve knit blouse with my one pair of white sandals with the wide heels. I had a white leather pocketbook with two outside strapped pockets that I had my traveler's checks in, a few singles and some change. I also had my big round prescription sunglasses, the height of fashion in the 1960's.

I remember my dark blue coat was heavy, meant for New York winters and not summers in Europe. The button was almost off. I had a worn short, lightweight red jacket but that was worse than the coat.

I decided to use my traveler's checks and buy a raincoat that would be perfect for my trip to Europe in the summer. I took the bus down Jamaica Ave. to Stern's and bought myself a raincoat. I remember as soon as I entered Stern's coat department I saw a mini-length, blue raincoat with a belt that would be perfect. I paid the salesgirl, with my first traveler's check, and told her I would wear it now. I put it on and as I walked out of Stern's I admired myself in the mirrors. I looked good, as would a well-dressed middle-class American on her summer vacation to Rome.

My mother, her two girlfriends and my sister gave me a big sendoff and they drove me to JFK Airport. My mother said she hadn't seen me look so good. The two friends asked if I packed the toilet paper. My sister said maybe next year we can go together. She was saving her money to move out to an apartment with a girlfriend.

Even though it was a nice sendoff I couldn't forget my mother had told me not to ask her for money if I got into trouble in Rome. I knew my mother had no money and couldn't help me out financially but why did she have to say it. It made it so definite. At least if it had not been said I could pretend that my mother would help me if I really needed it. I felt hurt and alone but tried to shrug it off.

When we headed out to the airport, I was the happiest I'd been in a long time. I didn't know if I was happy because I was finally going to Rome or because I finally was leaving where I had been living.

I remember when the propellers stopped and I landed in Iceland. I looked out onto the barren, flat, rocky land with wild goats and sheep wandering around.

The man who had been sitting by the window next to me told me he flew to Iceland many times for his work. He said they used Iceland for space travel practice because its barren land was the closest replica of the Moon's surface.

He had asked if he could put his feet up in the empty middle seat between us for the night. I had agreed but thought it was a little rude. He was interesting though, his information about space was quite informative.

When I reached the hotel room in Iceland, it was all white with straight furniture. A big quilt lay on the bed and it looked to be a mattress but felt soft and cushiony. In fact, I had thought it was a mattress and called down to the concierge to tell them that a mattress was left on the bed and the bed wasn't made. They assured me that was the way the bed was made.

I went shopping instead of going on a tour. I went to a novelty shop and started to buy. I picked up two little wood Viking ships with little round shields on the sides. I bought two heavy ribbed scarves that I found out later were really tablecloths. I still have one of the little ships. It was the first time in a long time I bought anything. I had it all sent home.

When it got late, it wasn't getting any darker. It doesn't get dark in Iceland during the summer. It got dark around midnight and only a twilight dark.

To this day, I remember what happened when I went down to dinner at the hotel. I was placed at a small table by myself when a waiter came over and asked me to please change my table and escorted me to a table with a young man already sitting there.

I was a little surprised but I sat down opposite the young man. He was a well-dressed young man on the handsome side and he spoke English. He introduced himself. I introduced myself cautiously and felt uncomfortable about the meeting. I didn't quite understand what had happened. Did this guy pay the waiter to put me at his table? It seemed that way. He was pleasant enough though. He talked of pleasantries and told me he was on a business trip. I told him I was on my way to Rome for vacation and to take art classes.

He paid for my dinner and walked me to my room. When we got to my room he talked his way in. He stayed the night but was a perfect gentleman. We didn't do anything I didn't want to do. For years after, I felt I had been used by him for a room for the night. Recently though, in my old age, I feel I was lucky he didn't rape me or beat me up and take my money.

Young girls, even if they think they can take care of themselves, are no match for a con artist, young, handsome man. Young girls are innocent, naive, and sometimes stupid about what can happen to them. They really do need to be taken care of even if they don't think so. Some older women are this way, too. I sometimes wake up in the middle of the night thinking about how stupid I was and mad at myself for being so naive. It was just luck I came out OK that night.

It was an uneventful trip back to the airport and onto the plane to Luxembourg. I was smarter in Luxembourg but still young and stupid. The room in Luxembourg had a balcony. I had never been in a room with a balcony before. I went out onto the balcony and looked down into the street.

I decided to wave to people. I waved at one woman who cautiously looked at me. Then I waved at another who waved back. Then a young man waved back at me and continued to walk down the street. Then about five minutes later he came back and motioned to me to come down. I thought this was funny and after all I didn't know how to get around Luxembourg by myself, so I went down. He spoke English and I remember we went for a walk and he told me about Luxembourg.

Luxembourg was, at one time, a castle and now has expanded to outer regions but you could still see the remains of the castle. He lived in Luxembourg with his family and knew four languages. He took me to a restaurant but all they served was horse meat. We had to go to another restaurant because I just couldn't eat horse meat. At the restaurant, the view was beautiful and I wondered what I was doing living in Queens when there were such beautiful places, such as this.

After dinner he lit a cigarette and invited me to go to his house. I wanted to see the inside of a European's house so I went. The front of his house had rounded cobblestone walls. There was a multi-colored spiral stone staircase up to the apartment. I remember a beautiful living room with ornate dark wood furniture and huge vases of flowers. It was nice to see flowers in the apartment. I wasn't used to seeing flowers in someone's house. I had never been in a house as that. It was so different from my mother's little Queens apartment.

His mother soon appeared. She was pleasant enough but she couldn't speak English. I remember thinking this boy would be appalled if he saw where I lived. I went to the bathroom and sneaked a peek at the dining room and part of the kitchen while heading back to the living room. The dining room table alone was the size of my mother's kitchen. It was dark wood with beautiful flowers as a centerpiece, the kitchen floors and countertops were made of marble.

If this boy really knew where I lived, he wouldn't give me a second look. I was not in his financial league. I guess he thought I was a middle-class American girl going to Rome on vacation. We had some cake then we left. I do remember slipping on the bottom step of that spiral staircase on the way down and was humiliated. He took me back to my hotel, told me to have a wonderful summer in Rome; kissed me goodbye and I never saw him again.

It was once said all roads lead to Rome and my life led to Rome. I arrived in Rome on Friday August 1, 1969. The Italian railroad had been worse than rush hour in New York. My ankles were swollen from traveling and carrying my suitcase. I just wanted to get to The Hotel Adriano and relax. The suitcases then did not have wheels, so you carried your suitcase. It was awful.

At the hotel, I was put in a single room with a shower. The hotel didn't have any air-conditioning but it seemed OK. I just remember hearing many noises because the windows were open. The bathroom had two toilets, and I wasn't sure what use one strange looking one was. The shower drain was flush with the floor and I almost thought the water would go all over the bathroom if I took a shower but it didn't.

Rome was a lot different from Luxembourg. It was ancient Rome, beautiful; it had culture everywhere you looked. It was old but it was artfully old. A thin little man about sixty or so was in charge of the student group for the Rome Institute. That night he took me to the café where the two girls I would be rooming with were. He told me I would be moving to their room in the morning.

We all introduced ourselves. One girl was an Army brat and the other was a doctor's daughter. I was really happy to meet them. I learned the doctor's daughter lived on Long Island. I guess I was hoping to make lifelong friends but that didn't happen.

They both had a different attitude toward boys and life than I did. They had met two Italian guys who were coming back with a third guy for me and we were all going out to a disco. When they came, we went to the disco. When we got to the disco we started to dance. Soon some other guys started to dance with us too.

A small fight broke out on the dance floor between the guys we came with and the new ones at the disco. It seemed an ordinary thing to these two girls but I was a little taken back by the commotion. I had never seen a fight break out before, especially one over me but it was over quickly, with the new dance floor guys winning.

These girls seemed to have an entitled attitude. They felt they should be fought over. They just thought they were something. I guess they were. They would be able to send a telegram to their parents and then have money wired to them. They didn't worry about money. Everything seemed to be handed to them and they expected it.

In time, they started leaving me out of things. I guess I didn't have the money to keep up with them anyway. I remember them going to get fettuccine alfredo at the restaurant Alfredo owned. I wanted to go with them but I didn't have the money and made some stupid excuse why I didn't want to go. They were also quite cruel at times, making fun of me. I remember I started hanging out with two teachers and a girl who were in the same hotel and the group.

I did go out with one of the guys from the disco. He seemed quite well off; he had a nice car and a summer house. I guess because I didn't go to bed with him we didn't go out for long. Looking back he was nicer than the guy I wound up with, during my time in Rome.

I met a few guys who all had cars except the one who I went out with for a few weeks. Why did I do that? Probably because he could speak English. I remember he was very nice at first then, toward the end, he actually hit me in public. I was very taken back and upset. He acted as if it were commonplace. I left a few days later to go back to New York, glad to be rid of him.

Guys in Italy liked young pretty girls. I guess who doesn't. During my trip, if I was walking alone guys would come up to me all the time. I found you had to walk with a man or an older woman to be left alone. Also the men wore tight shirts that weren't shown in New York until the next year. They were far ahead in fashion.

I did actually go to the classes at the Rome Institute for a while. I took an art history class. They were interesting, then most everyone stopped going including me. They were given early in the morning and most of us slept late. At that time, there was a siesta in Italy from 2 to about 6 o'clock; all the shops and places were closed. Everyone went home and rested. So there were no classes in the afternoon. Then, at about 6 o'clock, everything opened and started up again. When I went back to Italy years later, I was sorry there weren't any more siestas.

I had loved Italy. Rome was a beautiful, old, romantic city. I went to all the tourist places. The Vatican, Colosseum, Treve Fountain, Spanish Steps. I was young, healthy and ready to enjoy my trip and I did. It was the best trip I had when I was young. I went back to Italy a few times when I was older but it wasn't the same as it had been in my youth. The attractions had all sorts of security and fences. It was very sad to see the change.

I remember my mother and sister came to pick me up at the airport when I got back to New York. I was happy to see them but not happy to be back in New York. Everything looked old and worn and not where I wanted to be or live; but economics came into play. I had no money. I had to borrow a few dollars from my mother to get to work. I did give it back to her as soon as I got my paycheck. I resumed school at night, working during the day and life continued as it had been. There was nothing else to do but stay.

Chapter 18

Eventually, my sister moved to an apartment in the Bronx with a girlfriend. I stayed living with my mother, sleeping in the living room on the fold out couch. All my mother's girlfriend's daughters were getting married and moving out. My mother wanted her own life and seemed to be annoyed I was still there.

Her girlfriends would come over and would make sly remarks about me, such as your daughter ate all the chicken and who is she going out with now. I guess just being a twenty-year-old wanting to go out and do the things a twenty-year-old did annoyed her. Finally, my mother told me to leave.

I'm not sure what middle-class families do with their grown children living with them. Some let them live with them for nothing, some put them in their own apartments and pay the rent to get them out of the house. I guess some even take money from them and let them stay in the house. I wonder how many middle-class families tell their adult children who are paying them rent to move out. I guess some do.

I found an apartment with two other girls. We all had our own rooms and we shared a bathroom, kitchen and living room. So I moved. Actually, for the same amount of money I was giving my mother I would now have my own room and be able to do what I wanted. Come in whatever time I want. It actually turned out to be a good thing, moving out; however, I just about made it with money. It was always a struggle.

I stayed in that apartment for a few years. They were hard as well as easy years. I should have been on food stamps or something to subsidize my income. I barely had enough money for food some weeks.

I remember going to the supermarket and telling the cashier to add up the food items one by one and then telling her to stop when it came to the amount of money I had. One time, the cashier said she couldn't do that and just gave me all the food for the money I had. I hope she didn't get into any trouble. I said thank you very much and took the food.

Memories

I met my best girlfriend when she became one of my roommates. I'm still friendly with her and it's been about fifty years. She was an upper middle-class girl but we got along really well. Our friendship got us through many hard times. We had conversations until the wee hours, solved our problems and made each other feel better.

I had wonderful trips to her houses on Cape Cod and New Jersey. I met her fantastic parents. They were such nice people. Her father was the most wonderful man and father I ever met. We met each other's boyfriends and went out on double dates. She helped me with boyfriend problems and I helped her, until this day, we help each other.

I went out with a few guys. I didn't get married until I was thirty so I had a few boyfriends. Some of them were really nice and I let them go. Some of them were nice and they let me go. Some of them were not so nice and I kept seeing them. I guess we all have different kinds of romances.

I remember one time some guy broke up with me and I felt really bad. I told my girlfriend. She felt sorry for me. She was going to her family for the weekend and told me to come with her. She said it would cheer me up and I wouldn't be alone. I went with her and it was such a nice weekend. Her family was so nice and kind to me. She had an extended family that really cared for her and others. It made me feel so much better.

I also remember a guy taking me to a big barbeque. I guess it must have been Memorial Day, or Labor Day, or maybe the Fourth of July. I had never been to such an event. They had rows of barbecues with hot dogs and hamburgers, potato salad, corn, cakes and loads of other stuff. You took whatever you wanted to eat. There were many people playing games. Everyone was friendly and having a good time.

Usually, when I went out on a date with a middle-class guy, whatever we did, a barbeque or ice skating, or swimming, I didn't know how to do it or had never experienced it. This guy was shocked when I told him I had never been to a barbeque before.

A few years had gone by and Kenny was out of the service. He looked me up and we went out. I still didn't love him. Maybe it was because he just was so insecure. He came from a family of four kids who lived in a two-bedroom apartment. He slept on the pull out couch with his younger brother in the living room. His two sisters had a bedroom and his parents had the other bedroom. His father had been injured in WWII and one of his knees was fused together so he walked with a limp. His mother didn't work. His parents had paid to send him to college and he flunked out the first year. It just seemed to me I would marry someone who had the same situation I had. It really came down to I didn't love him and saw no future with him or, at best, an impoverished one. When he got out of the service, he even went back and lived with his parents.

I mostly went out with engineers that came from middle-class families. All the guys were becoming engineers in those days. I had my heart set on a college graduate from a middle-class family and for the most part that's who I went out with. Unfortunately, middle-class college graduates who were any good were scooped up by middle-class girls who had the same things to offer. The middle-class guys who went out with girls from lower incomes usually couldn't make it with the middle-class girls. At least this is the way I saw it.

Looking back, I don't think I knew how to act in a middle-class situation. You know the saying you can take the person out of the slum but you can't take the slum out of the person. In all honesty my personality at the time was not the happiest. I had a chip on my shoulder so maybe I scared off the good middle-class guys with my negative attitude. Who knows? I didn't have a positive attitude and that's what you have to have to get ahead. It's just very hard when you're poor and you don't have much. The people around you are usually not positive people either. You're taught to complain and feel cheated. You have to work extremely hard for the little you get. Even though it's exceedingly difficult to have a positive attitude but that's what you have to learn to have. You also have to surround yourself with people who will lift you up, support you and make you feel special. Sometimes these people are not your family and you have to get it from strangers. It's very hard to realize this about your family because they are all you have. All I knew was, I saw girls with their father's credit cards buying whatever they wanted and living in nice houses, not having to contribute half their salaries. I told people my father died when I was quite young, so I didn't have to tell them the truth. The truth was more damaging than the lie. People looked at you in a better way if your father died than if he just left.

I remember meeting a guy at a disco and one of the first things he asked me was what did my father do? I guess that said a good deal about a girl. I proceeded to tell him the truth but I should have lied. He didn't stay around to talk to me any longer. These middle-class girls easily got jobs through people their parents knew. They were treated with respect by guys. I felt I had to struggle for everything, do twice as much to get a job or buy something then get treated with less respect than the girls who got everything handed to them.

I once went to a job interview where a young middle-class girl was conducting the interview. I think the only reason she gave me the interview was to catch me in a lie. Her first question, said in a snobby way, was, "I see you put down you went to school and worked at the same time. How could you do that?" She was so upper-class she couldn't realize someone had to go to school at night and work during the day. She was surprised when I told her I went to school at night. It was as if she'd never heard of anyone going to school at night. I guess, in her world, everyone went to school during the day and had a fine time, while their parents paid their tuition until they graduated then got them a job. She asked me a few more questions and the interview was over. I didn't get the job. I regret not telling her off but I probably wouldn't have fit into her world, anyway.

I kept trying to go out with middle-class guys and hanging out with middle-class girls. Even though they were middle-class and came from money some of them were cheap, self-centered, and entitled; others were nice, generous and understanding. I guess you find that in all classes.

I did become engaged to a middle-class engineer, Jeff, who lived in Huntington in a beautiful house with his parents, sister and brother. I met him through a friend of my sister, who had gone out with him but said he wasn't her type. He wasn't handsome; he was tall and skinny and had a long face. My grandmother called him horse face. He didn't have a nice personality; he was bossy, not very supportive or nice to me. He didn't like it when I would help my mother and he would make comments about it. At the start of our relationship we talked about how we would see each other every week and we decided he would come to my apartment and I would make dinner for us. He acted as if he reluctantly agreed to this because I think he knew how one sided it was and how he really should have been taking me out but that's how we started dating.

At that point, I had very little self-esteem. I guess I felt I had to give whatever I could for a middle-class guy to go out with me. Also, my psychological problem with not accepting things because I was afraid there would be consequences came into play. It was almost a relief he wasn't taking me out to dinner because I felt psychologically there would be consequences for that. I remember my roommate saying to me he should be taking you out, not you having to cook for him every Friday. I continued to cook dinner for him every Friday, though; then, in the morning, he would take me out to breakfast on our way to his parents' house. We did hang out with some of his friends but never went out to a restaurant. I remember one time, we were at his parents' house on a Saturday night and we had dinner with them. After dinner he told me we were meeting some of his friends at a restaurant. I wasn't dressed to go to a restaurant and asked him why he didn't tell me. He shrugged. We got to the restaurant and his friends had all had dinner and we were there just in time for dessert. They were all out of the chocolate mousse, which I had wanted for dessert. Obviously, he didn't want to pay for dinner, he was so cheap. After all the dinners I made for him, I didn't have much money. Those dinners were a big chunk out of my food budget. I don't know why I continued to go out with him but I did and even was engaged to him.

The one thing I did get from him was a trip to Orlando, Florida. He wanted to see the launching of one of the Apollo missions so he booked a trip for us to go to Orlando. We saw the launch and we went to Disney World. It was just opening up. There was just one land built. I enjoyed seeing that. The trip with him was trying, though. He was not a fun companion; he would talk about a married girl he liked. A few weeks later, he broke up with me. I should have broken up with him long before he broke up with me but that is what happened.

Memories

This married girl and her husband were friends of his with whom we would go out. Her father was a principal of a school in Huntington. Of course, she got her teaching position in Huntington through her father. Her father met me a few times then asked me if I would take a position in his school. I told him thanks but no. I was so stupid. I didn't even realize it's the way of the middle class, getting positions for people they liked. I didn't know the ways of the middle class and lost many opportunities. Even my mother told me I should have taken it. I just felt I had to do everything on my own and not be indebted to anyone. How stupid.

I resumed dating. There was a married guy named Eddie who I didn't know was married. I met him at my favorite disco on Long Island. He was the most handsome guy I ever dated. He had beautiful blue eyes, blond hair and a body about which to dream. He would take me out to dinner and buy me flowers. There were no signs of him being married. I called him at his house, he stayed out all night and I met some of his friends. I went out with him for a glorious summer.

Then he told me he was married and his pregnant wife was coming back to New York with their child to have the baby. I burst out crying. I was devastated. I broke it off with him. A few weeks later I saw one of his friends and asked how Eddie was and his friend said married. I felt cheap for asking. Meanwhile his friends knew he was married when he went out with me, why didn't they say something then. About a year later, Eddie called me up wanting to see me but I was engaged to Jeff and told him he was married and I was engaged, and that was that.

There also was a guy with many psychological problems with whom I went out. He lived in a beautiful house on the North Shore of Long Island. He came from money but he just couldn't function. He couldn't sleep at night and would wake me up to go to the beach to get air in the middle of the night. I had to go to work the next day. I couldn't keep being awakened to go for a walk on the beach in the middle of the night. He had trouble holding a job because he needed to drink to be able to go to work. Of course, showing up for work drunk was not the way to keep a job. Finally, I broke up with him. I couldn't handle his problems anymore. A few years later, a mutual friend told me he had recently committed suicide. It was sad he never got well. I'm sure his rich parents tried everything they could to help him.

Then there was a nice middle-class guy. He was very pleasant and gracious. He took me to a friend's party once and the hostess licked the rim of the glass to put salt on it to make margaritas. Afterwards, I commented about that being a little germy and a few other things about the party. He seemed annoyed at my comments. He said it was very nice of her to have the party and stuck up for the hostess. I guess I shouldn't have criticized his friend because he didn't ask me out for long after that.

There were some lost opportunities with guys also. One summer I was doing a research project in a hospital. At one point, there was a young intern who came into the room I was in and started to tell me how he had no time to meet anyone. I don't know why this scared me and I walked out of the room. I almost went back in but I didn't. I think he was going to ask me out but I left. How stupid I was. I still could kick myself for that stupid move.

I remember I stood a guy up, not on purpose but because I forgot about our date. I had gone over to my Uncle Tommy's house. I would go over to my Uncle Tommy and Aunt Kay's house at least twice a month. They always fed me a good meal with many fun conversations. I would go over anytime I wanted. I didn't need an invitation; they always welcomed me.

When I got home my roommate told me the guy had come to pick me up and he waited a little while then left. I felt bad and stupid for forgetting the date and was going to call and apologize. I thought about what I would say to him. I don't think the truth would have helped him feel any better. I couldn't think of a good lie. I came to the conclusion I forgot the date because I wasn't really interested in him and the best thing to do was nothing. So I didn't even apologize to him. That was awful of me.

When I was still living with my mother there was a guy who came and picked me up for a Saturday night date. When he rang the bell, I came to the front door with my coat on and said we can go. He asked if he needed to introduce himself to my parents and I told him no there was no one home. My mother had gone out and I saw no reason to be in the house alone with him. So he took me to a disco and we had a good time drinking and dancing. I would have preferred dinner but I got dancing instead. He took me out about three more times and the same thing happened. I never let him in when he picked me up. I saw no point; my mother wasn't home. The fourth date when he came to the door he just about pushed his way into the house. He saw the little worn out living room, the one bedroom, and the small out of date kitchen. I was a little taken back. I was alone with him and he had just about pushed his way in. He took me to a disco and never called me again. I guess he didn't like what he saw.

There was the time my mother set me up. All I can say is, thank God I didn't come from a culture where the parents choose who you married. He came to pick me up in a nice coat and dress shoes. He was average looking, a little on the nerdy side. The only thing I can remember about him was he wore rubbers over his dress shoes. He had to take them off before he came in. Then a few minutes later had to put them on again because we were going out. *Who wore rubbers over their dress shoe? Maybe a Grandpa but not a young man.* The date couldn't have been very memorable because all I remember were the rubbers he wore over his dress shoes. I never went out with him again.

There was a guy with a Corvette. The car looked like something from outer space. When he came to pick me up he complained the bumpy streets were going to crack the paint on his car. This made me feel poorer than I was and more ashamed of where I lived. He took me out to the Hamptons once; to a house he shared with some guys. All they did was drink. I was starving. He never took me to get anything to eat. Between the remark about his Corvette's paint getting cracked, the drinking, and no food, I refused to go out with him anymore.

A guy from the old gang in Forest Hills called me and asked me out. He had never really been in the crowd I hung out with but I remembered him. I was living in the apartment we moved to after they sold the Forest Hills house. He came and picked me up on a cold winter's night and we took a bus to a bar. Not a disco but a bar; not even a nice looking bar. I was not a drinker and a bar wasn't my idea of a good date. He told me the kids in the neighborhood would talk about me and say I took the tip money and stole wallets. First I was shocked that he even brought up this stuff and even more shocked I was accused of something I never did. I did take the tip money once but never took anyone's wallet. Then I thought, why would he even want to go out with me if he thought I did all those things. Then it hit me; he took me to this bar didn't he? I ended the date and told him I wanted to go home. He did take me home. I never went out with him again. One thing I learned, you do one stupid thing, you get a reputation and then get accused of things you never did. You become the scapegoat for anything else of what people want to accuse you. I had ruined my reputation in Forest Hills because of one stupid thing I had done when I was thirteen. I decided not to see or talk to anyone in Forest Hills again. I hadn't seen anyone except for

Peggie anyway. She never mentioned anything about the tip money. I don't even know if she knew.

I once went out with a guy who was a teacher. We had teaching in common. At that point, I was teaching in a private school. I got my BA in Psychology instead of Education. I couldn't do student teaching because I was working in a private school as a teacher. You needed student teaching to get your BA in Education. I remember going to the Queens College counselor asking her if they would accept my teaching in a private school instead of me doing student teaching and she said no. I said to her, 'Who is going to pay my rent if I quit my teaching job to do student teaching. She just shrugged and I changed my major to psychology. Anyway, the teacher guy would make me dinner at his apartment. We went to his school's functions and I met some of his students and their parents. We went up to his house in the mountains which was fun. I thought something would come of the relationship, but it just fizzled out. I guess there wasn't any spark there.

Chapter 19

My mother always had arthritis but her arthritis started to get really bad and this started years of her being sick. She went to many doctors and tried a number of medicines. Years went by and she worsened. Soon, she was in and out of the hospital. Sometimes she was so bad she could hardly get out of bed. At that point, she was in the hospital at least three or four times a year. She was sick for over thirty years and every year she would be in the hospital.

I would work during the day; go to school Monday and Wednesday nights then visit her in the hospital Tuesday and Thursday nights and weekends.

When she got home from the hospital, sometimes I would stay with her. She would call me and I would go over if she needed me. Sometimes one of her friends would come over to help her. Once, her cousin came over but that was about it.

My sister had moved to Colorado with her soon to be husband Roger, and was going to school getting her Master's. She met Roger through me. We had both gone to our favorite disco and Roger's roommate had asked me to dance. We started talking and I asked him if he knew anyone for my sister. He then introduced us to Roger. I didn't really go out with the roommate but Roger and my sister hit it off. Roger was an engineer in New York and was soon transferred to Colorado. My sister went out there to live with him and to go to school. She married Roger in Colorado. I sent her a white bridal dress. She wanted a fashionable dress for the wedding. It was hard in Colorado to find the fashions you could get in New York. Eventually, Roger and my sister moved back east to Boston, where Roger went to law school while my sister supported them. He eventually became a very successful lawyer.

So I was left in New York to help my mother while my sister was in Colorado. I remember one time when my mother was in bad shape but I waited until my sister's test finals were over in Colorado before I told her. What could she do? She was in Colorado. I took my finals with the worry of my mother on my mind. This went on for years. At one point my mother asked me to come back home, quit school, and take care of her. I told her no. I guess this is not what she wanted to hear. She told family and friends how disappointed she was with me. I felt I was doing all I could but I wasn't going to give up my life.

One of my mother's girlfriends called me, the same girlfriend who didn't drive me home after Junior Achievement. She told me that my mother was seriously disappointed with me and I wasn't doing enough for my mother. I got really mad but instead of berating her, I said to her, "I don't do anything for my mother, right. Going to see her two nights a week and on weekends, taking her to and from the hospital, going to doctor's appointments with her, going over whenever she calls. I do nothing, right".

She quickly said, "Well I don't know if you do nothing but I know if it was my daughter she would be with me all the time". Until this day, I remember that.

*Who is she to judge me? Does she live my life and know what I am really going through? Instead of telling me I wasn't doing enough why didn't she do something. I try hard not to judge anyone who is taking care of a sick person. I know what it is and having everyone tell me what I should be doing and what they would be doing; yet no one helps me. They just talk about me and mostly what I am not doing righ*t.

My family wasn't much help but, at least, they didn't tell me they were disappointed in me. They would tell me what they thought I should do to help her, especially one of my cousins. They would tell me to call them and let them know what was

175

happening, especially when my mother was in the hospital. Sometime they would go to visit her in the hospital. When I did call them and tell them she was in the hospital or home from the hospital, some of them would act as if I were putting them on the spot to visit or help. So I stopped calling. I found the people who were really interested, called me when they wanted to know something. The other ones were just making conversation and acting as if they wanted to know and put it on me to call them, although no one came to help. I was the one who would take care of her, mostly.

I was exhausted between working, going to school, and helping my mother. I was just about wiped out. I had no energy for socializing. I was just about to give up and go back and live with my mother so I could take care of her. Now looking back, I know why I was engaged to the second guy. The second guy I was engaged to was someone I had broken up with when I was living with my mother, years ago. After going out with him for a year, Christmas came and he gave me nothing. Not to mention my birthday was December 28 and I also got nothing from him for that, either. I remember coming home from a date with him just before Christmas. I had given him a few things for Christmas. He just gave me a card and said he had told me he didn't want to exchange Christmas presents. My sister was shocked when I told her. Seeing her reaction, I knew this just was unacceptable. So I broke up with him.

I had been a little aggravated with him by that point anyway. I remember sewing a pretty pink dress for a New Year's Eve party. One of my girlfriends had invited us to a New Year's Eve party at her apartment. I had seen this dress on TV and knew I couldn't afford it. My mother helped me get the pattern and she helped me sew it. It had many detailed hand sewing. It took me a long time to do. I was looking forward to wearing it at the New Year's Eve party. He came and picked me up on New Year's Eve, never commented on my dress. We drove to the Bronx where the girl lived. When he got to her apartment building he said he didn't want to park in that neighborhood. He was afraid someone would steal his car. He drove back to my house and told me to call my girlfriend and tell her we weren't coming then he went home.

We had gone out for a year and he acted more as a brother than a boyfriend. He wasn't supportive or nice to me. He was critical and nasty. He would make fun of the way I looked, what I wore, where I lived and my mother. He acted as if I annoyed him. He was an engineer and he lived in a nice house with his parents. He was an only child and his parents spoiled him. Then he called me at the time when I was just about exhausted. So I started going out with him again against my better judgement. I guess I felt I didn't have the time or energy to go out and meet anyone, and he was there.

A girlfriend of mine told me she didn't like him and said she didn't think I should go out with him. So what did I do? I ignored her and didn't see her anymore. As the saying goes, love is blind. She was trying to save me from getting hurt but I wouldn't listen. Nobody liked him but I continued to go out with him. He finally got a job in New Jersey. He was living with his parents in Queens but the commute to New Jersey was too long to do every day. So he decided to move to New Jersey. I remember most of our dates consisted of buying furniture and getting things for his apartment in New Jersey. We would take long car rides to New Jersey. I remember going to a nice bar with him often. He didn't have many friends and my friends didn't like him, so we went out mostly by ourselves. He did have one friend who was married and we saw them a few times.

We never went to bed together. We would make out in his car and that was it. In those days some people would still say don't go to bed with a guy because they won't marry a girl with whom they go to bed. This was an old fashioned idea. It was the seventies and people were living together. This old fashioned idea was great for gay guys who didn't want to come out.

I now know this is with what I was dealing. He was an only male child in an Italian family. He could never tell his parents he was gay. Back then, many gay guys married girls just for a front. That's why I think it's so much better today. Let people say who they are and not pretend to be something they are not. This saves everyone a great deal of pain.

I guess since he was moving to New Jersey it was a good time to take a wife. I don't remember how he asked me to marry him but he did and I said yes. I felt to be a zombie. I didn't have any feelings; I just went along with everything. I was just depressed and exhausted. I guess I didn't even feel the nasty things he said and did.

He did give me a diamond ring. His parents met my mother and they started planning the wedding. His father asked if my mother had saved any money for the wedding. Of course, she hadn't. I said I didn't want a big wedding, not because it was the truth but because I knew we didn't have money for it. His father decided he was going to give his only child a wedding anyway and they booked a reception hall. I saved as much money as I could for the wedding but it wasn't much.

He got very nasty and mean right after he proposed. He would say things, such as 'your mother didn't even save for your wedding and now my father has to pay for it. Your mother will probably fall asleep during the ceremony'. He made fun of me and how I behaved. He seemed to go out of his way to say and do mean things. I think he wanted me to break it off. I was so sad and beaten down I just took it and went through the motions. I remember a friend of mine saying, "Are you sure he doesn't have some psychological problems?"

A friend of my mother's gave me a bridal shower. The same friend who didn't drive me home after Junior Achievement. She gave bridal and baby showers for everyone. She had a fairly nice house. Now looking back, it was a small Queens house with a living room, dining room and kitchen on the first floor, and three bedrooms and a bath on the second floor. Nothing really special about it but, as a child, I thought it was such a big, beautiful house.

My mother made me a white suit for the shower and I remember the jacket just didn't fit me right but I wore it anyway. He came to pick me up and when he saw me he said you have to buy clothes that fit you, not some junk that your mother made you. This is the way I went to the shower. At least my mother cared enough to try to make me a suit for the shower. If he really cared he would have bought me a suit. I actually had a good time at the shower. I got all the presents and it was nice being the center of attention. All the women made me feel better and happy. It was the only shower I ever had.

Eventually the day of the wedding came. The phone rang early that morning and it was his father. He told me his son was gone and left a note saying he couldn't go through with the marriage. Something was not natural about it. Later we found out he went on the honeymoon with his friend.

I went numb. I remember going over to one of my friend's houses and just crying and crying. Then I went to my mother's house and all my family was there. It was one of the worst days of my life. I could hardly talk. I had given up my apartment and my job. I had nothing, all the extra money I had saved I spent on the wedding. I couldn't understand how anyone could be so cruel.

Since I had no apartment or job it was decided I would go and live with my Aunt Kay and Uncle Tommy until I got on my feet. My mother was sick herself and couldn't take care of me. I was in a bad mental state. You could say, I had a nervous breakdown.

My mother did take me to a psychologist and I was in therapy for a couple of months. I did come to the realization there were signs; I just didn't want to see them. In a way, I let it happen to me. My Aunt Kay said if I had a father or brothers this would have never happened, they would have protected me from him. I agreed with her. I think they would have realized he was gay and got rid of him. My uncle said in a way he did me a favor. I would have been married to a horrible person.

My aunt, uncle and cousin helped me be settled. They took me to the jeweler to see if I could get any money for the ring, but the jeweler didn't offer me much. I was better off trading it in for other rings. I wasn't interested in doing that because I needed money. So girls, your diamonds may not be worth as much as you think. My aunt called up his father and made a deal that I would give back the ring for five hundred dollars. So I got five hundred dollars and they got the ring back. My aunt also knew a girl who was getting married and was looking for a wedding dress. She bought mine and I got some money from that.

It was a horrible time. Looking back, it was my own fault for letting him back into my life. I should have known I would have been better off without him but I was brought up that girls should get married. So I guess I just would take anything to get married. What a mistake. The first rule of a happy life is who you marry. So be very careful who you marry, especially the lower-class people.

Chapter 20

So, life went on at my aunt and uncle's house. I liked it over there. I enjoyed talking to my aunt and uncle. There was always dinner and someone was always home.

Then, in a few weeks, their youngest daughter came home with her baby. She left her husband. Now in the house were my aunt, uncle, me, my cousin, and her baby. Of course my aunt and uncle's attention went to their daughter and her baby. She left the baby often and went out. My aunt, uncle and I would babysit. I loved the baby and enjoyed taking care of her. I would take her to the park and for pictures with Santa. She was a joy to be around.

Eventually, I did start to get my life back. I started working in a math and reading tutoring school. I worked as a telephone solicitor. I even started going out again. My cousin would take me out to a local disco. When I saw my friends, at first they were quite nurturing but as time went by they would laugh at my being left at the altar. I guess it was funny. One of my friends once introduced me to some people and added that I had been left at the altar. I don't think she meant to hurt my feelings. I guess it was just a thing people enjoyed talking about. Soon other things became better gossip and my being left at the altar became old news. It still hurt though. It did change me. I think I became warier of guys and tried to be realistic about how they treated me and not be so naive and stupid.

After a while, my aunt and uncle decided I was ready to go off on my own. They had my cousin with the baby and had their hands full. I got an apartment in the next town over from them, in Babylon. I was having a tough time money wise. I was making it but just barely.

I actually started to meet some decent guys. I met one guy at a disco. From the moment he asked me to dance and took my hand, he made me feel special. I had never met anyone similar to him. He treated me with so much respect, bragged about me and just was so proud of whatever I was doing. He was just proud to be with me and he made me feel as if I were a goddess. Every Saturday night he would take me out to dinner, dancing and back to his place or mine.

We went out with his friends and mine. We had fun times together and we all liked each other. He just was always saying such wonderful things about me and to me. We even went and took hustle dance lessons together. I was never treated so special in all my life. That he was divorced with two children, paying alimony and child support was the only drawback. After going out for about a year we talked about our future and if we had one together. He said he would get married but didn't want any more children. I really couldn't blame him. He had two children. He was paying child support and seeing them every week. He didn't need more children. I, on the other hand, wanted to have children. I didn't want to be someone's stepmother and never have any children of my own. This difference slowly put an end to the relationship.

About that time, I had been working part-time in an insurance company and some guys had put in a new phone system. One of the guys was always talking to me and we had some fun conversations. When the phone system was done and the guys left, I got a phone call from him, asking me out on a date. I accepted. He was a very nice, kind, Brooklyn boy who was recently divorced with no kids. I was happy there were no children in the picture. He had his own business, installing phone systems. He wasn't a college graduate and he really wasn't middle class, even though he had enough money. He treated me nicely though, taking me out to dinners and movies. He was brought up in Boro Park, Brooklyn in a row house. Growing up he lived in the bottom apartment with his mother, father and two sisters. His two aunts and uncle lived in the top floor apartment. The apartments were exactly the same railroad rooms.

One of his aunts owned the building. He grew up poor but he had his aunts and an uncle that filled in money for anything he and his sisters needed. His aunts and uncle didn't have any children of their own. He and his sisters were the only children. He wasn't exactly what I was looking for but, by then, I was twenty-seven and very interested in getting married. I was living alone in the Babylon apartment, doing part time work and just about making ends meet. He once put chicken and steak in my refrigerator on the sly. I didn't know he had done it until the next day when I looked and saw it in the refrigerator. He did kind things such as that. I guess I needed it. He also lent me a car when mine broke down and I was saving to get it fixed. We started seeing each other every weekend. He would come to my apartment in Babylon and he would spend the weekend. Sometimes I would go to Brooklyn for the day. His father still lived in the first floor apartment. He went back and lived there with his father after his divorce. His mother had died when he was in his early twenties and his two sisters were married, now living on Long Island. His two aunts and uncle were very warm, giving people, when they realized he wasn't going back to his ex-wife and I was now the new girlfriend. They were Italian the same as me; I knew I had to win them over. I guess I did because they asked me over for dinner and it became a routine.

I liked his friends, and after the initiation they liked me too. I gave his best friend's wife some books for their children and they liked me well enough after that. My family and friends liked him too. My uncle actually knew him. He had bought some cars at the car dealership where my uncle worked. My uncle said he was a nice guy.

On Christmas Eve, I brought him to my Aunt Kay and Uncle Tommy's house. They would always have a big bash on Christmas Eve. They had moved to Farmingdale when my aunt threatened to leave my uncle if they didn't move out of Brooklyn. My cousin Gayla had been molested in the hallway of the building they lived in, so she wanted to leave Brooklyn and that horrible building. They were living in Farmingdale, Long Island now and having a good life.

My cousin Gayla had made many friends. Throughout the years, no matter where the friends lived, or how long it was since they were back to Farmingdale, they all stopped by my aunt and uncle's house on Christmas Eve. I even got to know them throughout the years. In fact, one of the guy friends was my usher at my cousin Sherry's wedding. My aunt decorated her house in green and red. Not the Christmas green and red but, at Christmas time, it really did look festive. My Aunt Kay would bake cookies, pies and cakes, and make the seven fishes while my grandma was alive. She also made special food for anyone who wanted something besides fish, and that was my boyfriend. She would make him a steak because he didn't like fish. My Aunt Kay came from Texas. She wasn't Italian, but she was the best Italian cook in the family. She also had the biggest heart in the whole world. She would help anyone out and make anyone happy, if she could.

I remember one Christmas Eve her septic tank was stopped up and she had to get a plumber. When she finally got one to come and he fixed the plumbing, she invited him to stay and eat with us and he did. He acted as if he were having the time of his life. My uncle was a happy-go-lucky guy and would tell jokes. He would make everyone happy and welcome. That was the best Christmas ever.

We started going over to my aunt and uncle's for Christmas Eve when my mother first married my stepfather. We had moved to Forest Hills about the same time my aunt and uncle moved to Farmingdale. I was in my early teens. There were many times it snowed so hard on Christmas Eve we almost didn't go because of the weather but we always got there. One Christmas Eve, we arrived there in a terrible snow storm and everyone decided to stay overnight. My other uncle and aunt were there with their families and decided to stay instead of driving home to New Jersey. My stepfather wanted to go home. It was a terrible night for driving and very dangerous. My mother wanted to stay. She actually stayed and he drove home alone. He did come back the next morning and said the drive wasn't so bad. That was one of the few times she didn't go along with what he wanted. Even after she divorced him, we would still all go over on Christmas Eve. My sister had married Roger and was in Colorado then Boston. She never went to those wonderful Christmas Eves after she moved.

Honestly, I had great Christmas Eves over at their house for almost thirty years. We started going over there when I was about thirteen, and it continued even after I got married and had my own kids. Actually, until my aunt and uncle died, we had Christmas Eve at their house. Even when it was just my aunt, she had Christmas Eve at her house. My uncle died around Thanksgiving and that Christmas she had Christmas Eve. I don't know how she did it but she did. They were the best Christmas Eves of my life. My aunt and uncle made so many people happy. They certainly made me happy. Until this day, if I get depressed about where I am at Christmas Eve, I remember those wonderful Christmas Eves and how lucky I was to have them for so long. I thank my aunt and uncle every time I think of Christmas Eve.

Chapter 21

I became engaged to the guy from Brooklyn. He asked me to marry him while we were camping at the Delaware Water Gap with my sister and her husband. We were canoeing down the river when he took out the ring and asked me to marry him. A canoe was a very interesting place for the proposal. He did think about how and when he would propose. The ring was a sapphire with diamonds all around it. He knew I liked sapphires and he knew I didn't feel diamonds were worth the money you paid for them. So he got me what I wanted. He was a thoughtful guy. He never made fun of me or got mad when I went to help my mother. In fact, he did the same. He helped his older father, two aunts and uncle, so he had the same situation as me. He was used to taking care of people. It was nice to have a person who felt the same way.

There were some drawbacks: he was bossy, didn't have a college education, and our love life wasn't too great. I was now twenty-eight and wanted to get married. I decided not to be too fussy. He was kind, relatively handsome, quite nice to me and my mother. My friends and family liked him. We were able to go out with all of our friends. It was just fun, nice and easy being with him. He made me feel good about myself and seemed to always help me and my mother. What more did I want? So we started making wedding plans. We looked at reception halls first. I found unless you were going to have more than a hundred people, you were going to have to pay more per person. I remember looking at a place right down the street from his best friend and wife. It was reasonable but it had gaudy speckled gold floors that just turned me off. We finally found Leonard's of Great Neck. It would accommodate us and we wouldn't have to pay more per person. So we booked Leonard's. On the whole, he was fine during the preparation and selection of things for the wedding. We both knew we would have to pay for the wedding. It wasn't even an issue that my mother couldn't pay.

I just remember one thing upsetting that made me wonder a little. We went to talk to someone about the wedding pictures. I asked a few questions then he told me to shut up. I was taken aback. I didn't know what to do so I shut up. He continued to talk to the woman as if I weren't there. Afterwards, I told him how rude he was and I didn't like it. He rather apologized. We picked a different place to get the wedding pictures, one that I knew was good from my photo spotting days but, unfortunately, after we got married that wasn't the last time he told me to shut up.

The engagement was mostly happy and fun. We went to his sister's house in Lynbrook and we would have barbecues. I got to know them and their two boys. They were fun people. His other sister lived in Lake Ronkonkoma and we went out to visit them and their three boys.

His best friend became his best man and we often went to his house in Brooklyn. They were wonderful, friendly people, generous and caring. I liked them even though they weren't college graduates. Some of them barely graduated from high school. We double dated with my girlfriends and went on vacations and camping with my sister and her husband.

I was now living in the upstairs apartment in my mother's house. It worked for me and her. I had lived in an apartment where the landlord lived on the bottom floor and I on the top. The landlord's wife would constantly come into my apartment when I was at work. Then, when I got home, I found she had tacked the shower curtain to the wall, lowered the temperature in the refrigerator or moved my clothes around. My drawers always looked as if someone had been in them and it wasn't me. I asked her not to come up to my apartment when I wasn't home. She said she had a right to make sure I didn't leave the windows open or did something that would damage her house. I put a lock on the door that only I could open. She had a fit and told me to take it off. I refused. The turning point was when they didn't give me enough heat. I put the oven on for heat. I guess they saw the gas meter when the oven was on for a while and the husband started banging on my door screaming turn the oven off. He was banging and screaming as a maniac. I called the police. When the police came, the landlord and his wife had turned off all the lights in their apartment and pretended not to be home. I knew I wasn't dealing with rational, normal people and decided to move.

Just about that time, my mother's upstairs apartment became vacant. I asked her if I could rent it. I guess she felt she needed me close by to help her and told me yes. It mostly worked out. She was a little bossy though. I paid her rent but when she didn't approve of the way I spent my money she would tell me. She did this when I decided to foster a Worldwide child in need. It was eighteen dollars a month. I told her about it, she got very mad and said if I could do that, I could pay her more rent. I stopped telling her what I was doing with my money. I remember one Christmas I had made Christmas butter cookies and some carolers came to the door. I decided to give them some cookies and I brought the tray down to the front door. My mother said no and just about grabbed the tray from me. I did give the carolers the cookies but I didn't understand why my mother tried to stop me. For the most part, though, it was fine. I helped her when she needed something. I sometimes went down and had dinner with her. Also, when friends and family came over we all had a nice visit. I wasn't lonely there. I got to know the neighbors. Overall, it was fine.

I was teaching then. I had a part time kindergarten teaching position in the morning and a part time daycare teaching position in the afternoon. Teaching jobs were hard to get at that time. I couldn't get a full time teaching position so I worked two-part time positions. The kindergarten position was in a Catholic school so they didn't pay much. They also asked me to do things in addition to what the job required. They once asked me to drive a nun to the George Washington Bridge to meet someone. I don't know what that had to do with my teaching; it sure was inconvenient. They didn't give me gas money or any other assistance. I also had thirty children in the kindergarten class which was too many kids for one teacher. I now know that was illegal. Now they only have eighteen in a class. I think they still stretch that rule. Even the public schools find ways of getting around the legal number of students in a class. If you are an untenured teacher, what are you going to do?

The afternoon position was at a daycare in an all-black area. I remember walking in the street and some black boys throwing snowballs at me. After that, I always tried to park close to the daycare and never left once I got there, except to go home at the end of the day. All of the students were black and about eighty percent of the teachers were too. For the most part, they were nice to me. One teacher told me she used to feel when things went wrong in her life it was because she was black. Then she became aware that white people had the same problems she had. It wasn't because she was black. I did make the mistake once by asking a black teacher about her husband. I got a lecture on just because you have children with a man doesn't mean he is your husband. So I got a good taste of the different cultures.

The manager of the day care was OK but a little strange. I put on my application I had a BA It was in Psychology not Education but I did have a BA. She asked me if I really had a BA because she checked. I told her I really had a BA and she did check. She thought I was lying about my BA. Some of the teachers told me I had more education than most of the teachers there. There was a policy that one teacher had to stay late and wait with the children whose parents came late to pick them up. Every day someone was late. They wouldn't pay you for staying late. Sometimes you waited for a half hour or more. I think nowadays the parents have to pay if they are late.

The children were cute. I felt sorry for some of them. One little boy would be in daycare until 6 o'clock then someone would pick him up and take him to another daycare until 8 o'clock. Some children would come and say it was their birthday and the parents did nothing for the child's birthday. The teacher would bake a cake and make a party a class project. Most parents would bring in cupcakes for their child's birthday.

Just before the wedding, I got a full time teaching position in a Catholic school close to my house. The nuns and teachers were wonderful. Most of the teachers were the same age as me. Some of them were engaged too. We had a lot in common. We all started going out as a group. Even after we had children, we stayed in touch. One of them is still one of my closest friends.

I didn't have a wedding shower because I had one already when I was engaged to the guy who left me at the altar. I did give back all the gifts but still we decided not to have another shower. The guy I was marrying was divorced, so why put his family through another bridal shower. The wedding was going to be enough. So the only shower I ever had was the one I gave back all the gifts. In my mind this was fine; I didn't like getting things from people. I still had psychological problems about that. Of course, the list for the wedding was a little tricky. Everyone wanted us to invite certain people. I just remember my cousin Gayla asking if she could invite a boyfriend. I said of course she could. I wasn't going to have anyone come to my wedding alone unless they wanted to.

I remember my mother's girlfriend, the one that didn't drive me home that one night from Junior Achievement, not letting me bring anyone to her daughter's wedding. I asked her if I could and she said no. She let my sister bring Roger because they had been going out for a while. They weren't engaged, just going out for a while, about a year. First, I felt because we were twins we should be treated the same and get the same invitation. Second, how could she expect me to go alone to the wedding when my sister was bringing someone. So I made an excuse and didn't go. My mother felt I was wrong. I felt I was right. I wrote a letter to Dear Abby and asked what the proper thing was in this case. After a year, I got a reply saying I was right to expect to be treated equally to my sister.

We continued to invite people to the wedding and make plans. My mother was busy making little fabric roses that were filled with rice. I would go downstairs and we would sew the long tubes of yellow material then cut them into sections and tape them to the wire, material roses. Then we'd filled them with rice and put them in a basket. They were given out to everyone outside the church after the wedding ceremony and everyone threw the rice at us and kept the flowers.

The wedding drew near and it was time for me to pick up my wedding dress. My dress and veil cost three hundred dollars. It was a Saturday. When I went to the store I had one hundred fifty dollars in cash, and I was going to give them the rest in a check. They wouldn't take my check. So I drove back to my mother's house and she took my check and gave me the cash. In those days, there were no ATM machines. If the banks were closed, they were closed. You had to make sure you had the money you needed before the weekend. A neighbor let me put the dress on the bed in one of her spare bedrooms, which was really nice of her. This way it wouldn't be wrinkled. I remember laying it out on the bed; it looked so pretty.

The wedding took place on a hot July day. They had brownouts then, which meant not all the electricity was going to the appliances. So the air conditioners blew cool air but not as cold as it should have been. The brownout was supposed to stop you from getting a total blackout, which meant no electricity at all. Also, because we lived in a heavily populated area there was no water pressure. On hot days, when everyone was using water, you got very little water coming out of the faucet. I remember taking a shower in a little trickle that day.

Most of my family came. They came from Pennsylvania and New Jersey. My sister was my matron of honor. We both were excited about it. She had married in Colorado and never really had a wedding. So my wedding was the wedding we both got.

We were married in an Episcopalian church right near my mother's house in Ozone Park. It was a pretty church. The pastor had a wife and two daughters. One of the daughters had spina bifida and walked with crutches. We made friends with the people at the church. There were a few couples our age and we used to go out with them. We once organized a wonderful Valentine's Day dance at the church. We all decorated the church basement and made the menus and got the food. All our friends and family came. Between the new friends at the church and the old friends we had a great time. There was a band and we all danced and ate and just enjoyed ourselves. The members of the church said they couldn't remember ever having a dance like that at the church.

Chapter 22

So we were married in the friendly Episcopalian church on a hot July day in 1978. We had an organ playing. I put a bouquet on the Blessed Mary's altar for an extra blessing. We had extra flowers on the altar and flowers around the pews. My bouquet was all white with roses, stephanotis and baby's breath. My sister had blue and yellow flowers in her bouquet. The men wore light yellow jackets My sister, my only bridesmaid, wore a lovely blue flower dress with a big brimmed hat. My mother had a beautiful blue dress, which my friend helped her buy a few days before the wedding. She was going to wear a plain, long dress which I didn't like. I was so glad when her friend talked her out of it and she got a new one. Everyone looked really nice. Everyone was happy. My Uncle Tommy walked me down the aisle. The ceremony was lovely, even if everyone was hot.

After the ceremony, we got into the limousine and went to Marcy Photo Studios to have our pictures taken. Everyone went back to my mother's house to wait until it was time to go to the reception. I felt so special being in the limousine. We even went back to my husband's house to pick up his uncle who had refused to go to the wedding. His father had died about six months before the wedding from a stroke. His two aunts were at the ceremony with his two sisters and their families. His uncle didn't like leaving the house so he didn't come even when we went to pick him up in the limousine.

We drove to Leonard's for the reception. Leonard's was a big reception place with several weddings going on at the same time. We decided to go to the cocktail hour. At that time, the custom was the bridal party did not go to the cocktail hour. They would make a grand entrance at the beginning of the reception. I guess we felt we were paying for it and we wanted to experience it all. The cocktail hour was wonderful. We even had a hot dog stand, which was a popular touch. The reception was more than anyone could want. The priest who had married us gave a blessing and gave us a Russian icon for a gift. We had a band that could even sing in Italian. Everyone danced. The food was great, at least, I thought so. We even had a Viennese hour, which consisted of all kinds of desserts, including the wedding cake. That was fun, especially because I love desserts. They wheeled all these desserts out on tables with big flaming candles. We all gathered around and picked what we wanted, including the wedding cake. It was a big hit.

When the reception was over, we opened all the envelopes to see how much money we had received. His family had been very generous. His aunts gave us five hundred dollars. One of my mother's friends had been very generous, giving us more than my mother. My mother gave us seventy-five dollars. I was a little shocked by this. Later, my sister told me my mother felt she had been giving me money by not charging me much rent. I felt she should have charged me what she thought was the right amount for the rent because it looked as if she didn't give us very much for the wedding. My husband didn't think anything of it. He was very kind and never said anything bad about my mother. Now I realize my mother did what she could. I try to think of the wonderful things she did for the wedding. She spent hours making the yellow material roses in which to put the rice. She had been there to help with all of the preparations. It's better to just dwell on the good someone does.

The next day, we started on our honeymoon. We were originally going to go to Canada, but one of my friends gave us a week in a little cottage on Cape Cod as a wedding present. So we went there. I had spent many a trip with my girlfriend there. We had wonderful times hiking and swimming or going to the sand dunes near P Town. It was a lovely little guest house next to the big house on a lake in Dennis.

When we got there a county fair was in full swing. They had horse pulling contests, rides, and games. My husband won a stuffed animal for me in a shooting game. I forgot what I did with it. It was a special thing to have been given on my honeymoon.

One night, we got back to the guest house and there was my sister and Roger sitting in the living room. They now lived in Boston where Roger was going to law school. They had been to the guest house a couple of times so they knew where it was. Roger had just finished his finals and they wanted a vacation. So they stayed in the guest house with us and we continued to enjoy our honeymoon with them. It was funny because they let themselves into the house. They opened a window and crawled in. So they were sitting in the living room when we got home.

We were all young and healthy then. We all got along. Cape Cod was an unblemished place. There weren't crowds of people. We would drive along and decide to have a picnic, stop, just place the blanket on the ground and bring out the food, eat and enjoy. We bought lobsters and boiled them. Sailed boats on the lake, swam in the ocean. We had rubber rafts we filled with air and put into the canals and just floated around. We even took a small propeller plane ride around the Cape; scary, but fun. It was glorious. Roger was the smartest of us all. He knew a lot about the history of Cape Cod. He was brought up in Boston by upper middle-class parents. He also was just plain smart. If he went somewhere once, he would remember how to get there again. It is no surprise he became such a successful lawyer.

My husband was the nicest and most easy going of all of us; He also was very mechanical and could fix anything. I don't remember what my sister and I were. I do remember being afraid of all the aqua life in the water. When we saw a stingray and I didn't know what it was. It looked pretty scary to me. I also was afraid of little crabs but I loved Cape Cod. It was a wonderful honeymoon. The week went by fast and we returned to live in the apartment above my mother. Everything was about the same. I worked in the Catholic school not far from the house. He drove back to Brooklyn where his security supply store was located.

After work, I would go to the store and help my husband with accounting. I would call up customers who didn't pay their bills and ask them to pay. I felt if they owed a certain amount they should have to pay the bill first before they got more credit. My husband didn't feel this way. I would see customers come in and buy twenty thousand dollars' worth of equipment and put it on credit when they already owed twenty thousand. I didn't think this was a good way of doing business. Soon he hired an accountant and I didn't have to go anymore. It's not good enough to know how to market a business and bring the customers in. You also have to know how to handle the money. How to make sure you got paid. I don't think my lower-class husband knew how to do this. I think he needed a middle-class partner to help him get his money and stop giving credit.

We were also very active in the church where we were married. There were two other couples we hung out with often. We had many fun times doing things for the church. Then something awful happened. One of the girls had an affair with the pastor. It was a shock. Everyone found out. We all thought the husband was going to do something to the pastor but he didn't. Meanwhile, the whole church was disrupted. It was a little church just hanging on anyway and this just about put it over the edge. The pastor was fired. His wife divorced him and went with her two girls to live with her mother. The pastor and the girl eventually got married and had a child. It just broke up the whole congregation.

When the new pastor was hired, there came another awful event. A beloved member of the congregation, while helping them move in, had a heart attack and died. This was just heartbreaking. It totally broke up the church especially that the new pastor just kept on unpacking—he didn't even go to the hospital with the man when he was having the heart attack.

The church was not the way we knew it. It was time to move on.

she had the same due date as me. We saw them a few times. After I had my daughter I came upon the same woman sitting outside her house with her baby boy. That started our friendship.

I was thrilled with my daughter. She was everything I wanted. My husband was thrilled too. It was interesting, people asked him if he was disappointed he didn't have a boy and he wasn't. He was just happy to have a healthy baby.

I did have to have a C-section and the doctor cut the baby on the cheek. Luckily, it didn't leave a scar. I didn't enjoy being pregnant. I was glad I was able to get pregnant and have a baby but I really didn't feel well during the pregnancy. I found the delivery was very long, hard, and the most painful thing that I had to go through in my life, except maybe a bad gallbladder. I was actually happy when they said I was going to have a C-section. I was in so much pain I just wanted the pain to stop.

She was just beautiful, and a really good baby. She slept through the night when she was three months old. She was an easy baby. She was on time or advanced in the growing learning situations. I loved her more than anything I ever loved. The happiest times in my life were when I was home with her. There is no way to describe the love I had for her. I guess only being a mother yourself, you would understand.

The first year was an adjustment. I remember loving being home with her. I was so glad I didn't have to go back to work and leave her with someone. She was my world but I was a little lonely. I did start to make play dates with the women I had met and that helped. Every week we would go to each other's house and the babies would play and we would enjoy each other's company while exchanging ideas about baby care. A third girl joined us with her baby boy who had been born on August 3. So there were the two baby boys born August 3 and there was my baby girl born August 4.

I would also drive to see my mother once a week. She only lived about a half hour away. We also visited my husband's two aunts and uncle in Brooklyn. We had many friends and family close by. It was wonderful.

I hope I appreciated it at the time. It just seemed that's what Italians did. Everyone lived near each other. No one moved out of the state for a better job. Children stayed near the parents and the parents enjoyed their children and grandchildren. I now know how very lucky I was. There was plenty of help and love nearby at all times for everyone. That's one thing the lower class seems to know, they seem to know to stay close to family.

Two years later, my son was born. He was an easy birth; my water broke just before we were going to eat pizza with my husband's family. Of course, I couldn't eat it. I had to go to the hospital. My husband had to go get my mother, whom he had just driven home. She was to stay with my daughter while I was in the hospital. My son was born by C-section with no labor. He was a big baby who liked to eat. He did not lose weight in the hospital, as most babies do.

Memories

I was now home with my two children. I loved it. I was very fortunate my husband made enough money for me to stay home with the children. I was now getting into a middle-class situation. Who you marry is very important for your happiness. They were the happiest days of my life. The two of them were so cute. I can still see them running to the door to greet their daddy when he got home from work. My daughter was a lovely bright child. She did well in preschool. I wanted to give her everything. My son was a beautiful baby. He was laid back and just liked to sit and watch everyone. He was a thinker.

I would take them to the local little parks and push them in the double stroller for walks. I would have play dates with the two friends who now had their second child also. We would enjoy large family holidays. It was a happy time in my life.

My daughter, Susanne was a mature child right from the start. She seemed to understand more than a child her age should. She was articulate. In preschool, she would do her project and help another child do his or hers. In kindergarten, the teacher told us she was advanced. I did teach her at home and by the time she was two and a half she knew all the letters of the alphabet. She would watch Mister Rogers' and Sesame Street. She made many friends in school and in the neighborhood. There were her two boy cousins living around the block, and their cousin living across the street from us. In school, she was put in the exceptional student program and was given extra lessons. She did well in all her classes. She usually was the teacher's pet. I remember going to the school and seeing her class in the hallway and there she was holding the teachers hand with a couple of other little girls in the front of the line.

She was the lead in the school play in fifth grade. She played Little Red Riding Hood. My mother made a beautiful costume for her. We all went to see her in the play. She was an extrovert and she loved being the center of attention. She played the clarinet. She was in the choir. She loved doing extracurricular things. She wanted to do everything. In junior high, she had the lead in the school play *The Little Mermaid*. She was on the debate team. She started getting into sports. She was into track running and volleyball.

In high school, she started narrowing down her interests. She started keying in on the sports. She became a really good track runner and volleyball player. We used to take her to her meets and she would win many of them. Her name would be in the high school sports section in the newspaper. Not only did she take the AP courses she also took the IB courses in high school. She always did well in her classes. She pushed herself to do well. She hung around with a nice group of kids in high school. Mostly they didn't get into any real trouble.

She got a scholarship to Holy Cross College for track and academics. So she decided to go there. It was a wonderful school. She even studied in Oxford, England for a year. We went to visit her in England and it was fascinating. We went to a hall where the students would eat and it looked like something out of a Harry Potter movie. Oxford is not just one school. There are many schools in the town of Oxford. She went to Manchester.

When she graduated from Holy Cross, my mother was still alive and able to go to the graduation. It was the last event she was able to go to before she died. We had a big college graduation for Susanne at the house. She then got a job in Manhattan as a paralegal. After a few years working as a paralegal she decided to go to law school. She was accepted into San Diego Law School. She was there one year and transferred to George Washington. Yes, you can transfer in law school; I think only in the first year. She is now a partner in a law firm.

She met her husband in law school in San Diego. He transferred to Harvard. They had a long distant relationship while going to law school. They now have two beautiful children, a girl and a boy. I'm a very happy grandma.

My son, John was just what I wanted. I wanted a boy and I got a boy. He was so cute. He looked as a cabbage patch doll. He was a bald and chubby little baby who liked to eat. He was in the 90th percentile in height and weight on the doctor's growth charts.

He was a thinker and a watcher. You could put him down on a blanket with some toys and he would happily stay there and watch what everyone was doing. He was a real child. He had childhood fears and misconceptions. He really thought he could go down the drain in the bathtub when he was taking a bath. We had to sing Mister Rogers' song, *Only the Water Goes Down the Drain*. He loved to watch the garbage trucks when they came to our street. He loved Superman the most. I bought him Superman pajamas until he was about ten; then Superman t-shirts.

When he started preschool he loved it. Then in about two months he decided he didn't want to go anymore. So the teacher had to carry him in crying. He did well in preschool. He was smart. He just didn't want to go. When he started kindergarten, he was in the same class as his best friend who lived around the corner but the teacher still had to carry him in crying for a little while. He did well in kindergarten. The teacher would let the parents come in and help. I did a few times and he was fine. He did the work and was happy. He was very talented in music. He eventually started playing the piano and the guitar. Until this day, he is very talented in that.

I saw him in the hall when I went to visit his elementary school and he was one of the boys at the end of the line fooling around. His teacher was leading the line out of the classroom and everyone was in a nice line. I kept looking for my son and finally, when everyone was out of the classroom, there came my son and a few other boys playing around at the end of the line. That was my son.

I taught him religion for his confirmation and he easily did the work then laughed with anyone who was joking around. He just did the work he needed to do with ease. He didn't do any extra. He never started fooling around but he was one who laughed with the ones who were.

In junior high, I went to visit him in music class. The class was being taught the guitar and he just was so far ahead of everyone in the class. He really had musical talent. The students took turns playing the same piece then, when it was my son, John's, turn he played it perfectly and so much better than any of his classmates.

In high school he was very talented in technology. He quickly knew what to do with a computer. At that time, all of the new technology was starting and he knew how to use it. He seemed to catch on fast and was able to do things I didn't even understand with computers.

He had some nice friends. One friend would go to Italy every summer to his grandparents and, a few times, my son went with him. He got a taste of living in Italy. Some summers he would go up and stay with my sister in Islesboro, Maine. He loved running around with his cousins and with the kids on the Island. He was a free spirit. He was a boy and he would get into trouble with driving and cars. On the whole he was a good teenager. He didn't give us too much trouble, for a boy.

He started Niagara College and one year he went to Ireland for a semester. We went to visit him. Ireland is an enchanting country. It is mystical, with leprechaun and fairy mounds. The people are easy going, very creative and imaginative. It was a beautiful trip. He worked in castles and learned the ways of the Irish.

He became a successful IT person. I don't understand what he does but it's important and he makes a good living. He has a wife and they gave me my first beautiful grandson.

I tried to bring my children up middle class. Luckily, we had enough money. We had to get a second mortgage but we were able to have enough money to send them to college and do things that middle-class kids do. I also went back to work as soon as my children were in school full time so we could have extra money. Even with that it was hard keeping up in Rockville Centre on Long Island but we did. The children came first.

Sometimes my old, lower-class ways would seep in but I was willing to change and do what the middle class was doing. I remember when my daughter was going off to college; everyone was into buying stuff for their college bound child. For some reason, I didn't think it was that exciting and I thought she could buy stuff on her own. With the money I gave her, of course. I was quickly shown how all the mothers went with their child to the store. So I changed my tune and went to the store with my daughter. We let them both go to colleges away from home. This is a very middle-class idea. Most lower-class people keep their children near them.

We never asked our children for money even if they had paying jobs. I never asked them to work while they were in high school. In college, they had summer internships or paying jobs. I never asked them to give me half their salaries. I wanted them to experience and learn things in their childhood. I would have them go and be in plays at school because I knew being in front of people would make them more comfortable in adulthood. I gave them parties and let them get used to getting gifts and being the center of attention. I also made sure I didn't put the female restrictions on my daughter with which I grew up. I remember I bought her a fire truck when she wanted it. Some people didn't think I should have done that but I wanted her to know she could be whatever she wanted to be, even if she wanted to be in a male profession. I tried to do the same with my son. I tried to treat them equally.

When my children were growing up, it was nice being around family, especially during the holidays. Everyone was close to one another and there to help if you needed it. Even if someone lost their job and could get a better one outside the area, they didn't. I don't know if that was good or bad. It did keep people back, career wise. This is what lower-class people do. They stay close to family but, somehow, people survive and another job comes along.

The first ones to leave the family were considered rebels. My sister first moved to Colorado then Boston with Roger. One cousin moved to Minnesota then to Connecticut. At that time, they only moved for the husband's career. Both husbands made a good deal of money and climbed the ladder.

The ones that stayed didn't fare as well. Then again, maybe those husbands would have done well no matter what. Neither of them originally came from the area, anyway.

In those days, women's careers were not considered important. The most important thing a woman could do was marry a husband who had a good career and future. That was really her career. If a woman went to college she was going to be a teacher or a nurse. Those were the careers that were open to her unless she had a man who was going to protect her in another field. Before the seventies, women weren't even allowed into certain colleges.

Of course, things have changed. Women are allowed into most colleges. The colleges lost much funding if they didn't matriculate women. It is wonderful that a woman can become a lawyer, engineer or doctor nowadays; or just about anything she wants. She can practically work in any field in the United States and most of the other countries of the world. The pay isn't equal to a man's but it is a whole lot better than it was when I was young.

One of the things that changed was the closeness a family had in those days. Now that I'm older and living in Florida, I miss the closeness of the family. When I was growing up, there were children, grandchildren, even great-grandchildren around in one area. As you got older, you were able to appreciate them all.

Having your own children is the most wonderful thing in the world. Not even grandchildren can compare. You may love your grandchildren as much as your own children but they are not yours. If their parents decide to move far away then the grandchildren go with them.

You love your children more than anything or anyone. Also, you love your children more than they love you. It sounds cruel but that is the way it is. That is the way it should be. When they are young, until about ten or so, you are their world. That is when they love you the most. No other time will they love you as much.

They need you, they want to please you, they want to imitate you. You will hear them telling stories all the time "Mommy said and Daddy said"; you are everything to them. That is when you have your most important family, your nuclear family. That is when you mold them for their adult life.

Then they hit teenage years and you are not their world anymore. Their friends are. This is a very dangerous time. They imitate their friends. They want to please their friends. As all teenagers, they are worried about fitting in; and their friends just really care about themselves fitting in. This is when some teenagers die, doing things to be accepted into the group. They want to please the group so this is when they will get into a car or drive a car drunk. This is when they will do sexual activities just to be accepted and liked. Most teenagers are not mature enough to really care about others or know what is best to do.

There have been teenage parties where a teenager has fallen down the stairs and was just left lying there because none of the others knew what to do or was afraid to call the police or an ambulance.

They were afraid of getting into trouble themselves. They can be very self-centered at that age. They are not adults; they still react like children. They may look to be adults physically but they are not. At that point, you have a very tough parenting job with your teenager.

Then they make it to college age. Most of the affluent ones go on to college. At that point they usually feel very entitled and ready to leave you. They are happy to get away from home. They think they know it all and they will do much better without you and all your rules and regulations. So you send them off to college, which costs you a small fortune. Middle and upper-class society instilled in everyone that the child is entitled to go to the college of their choice, and the parent is obliged to pay.

At first, when they get to college, for the most part they love it. Until they get sick and no one takes care of them or their roommate tells them they can't sleep in the room tonight because her boyfriend is going to be there and they have to find a place to sleep for the night or a host of other awakening things come up and life away from home becomes a reality. Some transfer to a college close to home and come back home, others stick it out. No matter what, they all get a taste of what life is about without the protection of home and parents.

There are a few things that happen after the four years are up and they graduate. Some decide they prefer being a student and persuade their parents to pay to send them to graduate school. So they stay students and continue to live off their parents. Some even persuade their parents to pay for their doctorate.

The ones that graduate from college and come back home either get jobs their parents get for them or they just seem to not be able to get a job for a long time. No job is good enough for them. They just are not going to stand for a lower paying job that asked them to do things that are beneath them.

Some get jobs in what they majored in and decide they don't like it and want to go back to school and major in something else. Some actually get a job, stick to it or change jobs until they find what they like. Then they move out and get their own place.

This is a time of how much money the parents are willing to give to their children to let them find themselves in the world. Some spend much money. Some even put their child, and pay the rent, in their own apartment. The child or should I say young adult seems to not want to abide by the rules of the house when they get back home, so the parents put them in their own apartment.

This is great, the child gets their own free apartment so they can do whatever they like and they don't have an incentive to get a job. I guess this works for the parents too, they indirectly keep their child dependent and thus postponing their child's becoming an adult, keeping them near the parent. It also postpones the child from getting married and starting a family, unless they find someone who is willing to be controlled by the parents' money also.

There are many different scenarios that happen after the middle-class and upper-class child graduates. I came from the lower class, so I know what happens when a lower-class person graduates; not from college, but from high school. They are expected to go to work and contribute to the house. I'm not saying this is the way it should be. In fact, I don't really think that's the way it should be but there should be something in the middle. The pendulum swinging to the extreme in either direction is not good. Finding a middle position is the key. I guess every family has its own middle position. It could even be different for each child.

I remember asking a teacher I worked with, who had children a little older than mine, "When do you stop giving your children money?" She replied, "When you decide to".

Chapter 24

I now had two children and lived in Lynbrook in a cute little Cape Cod house. When my son was born we raised the roof, literally, and made four bedrooms upstairs. So now each of my children had their own room and we had a spare bedroom for guests. Downstairs was a kitchen, living room, dining room, and den.

Life seems to go in stages. There was the early childhood stage, the teenage stage, young adult and on your own stage. This was the children's early marriage and family stage. This was probably the happiest time in life for me. I didn't have to go out to work, I was at home with my two children. I didn't have to worry about the mortgage or the food bill.

My husband was a good provider. I was happily raising my children with plenty of friends and family around.

Unfortunately, there were signs the marriage was headed for trouble. Our parenting skills were not in sync. He wanted to be their friend more than an authority figure. If I said they couldn't have cookies until they finished their dinner, he would sneak them cookies. I made balanced meals: chicken, potatoes, vegetables then dessert. I would ask the kids what they wanted and tried to make what they would eat. Sometimes they would eat and like a meal then the next week refuse to eat the same meal.

My husband would blame me if they didn't eat. Saying I didn't cook what they liked. It had to be a battle and sometimes I felt no matter what I cooked, it wasn't going to be the right thing. So I told my husband if he and the children didn't like what I cooked, he could cook for them.

He did cook for about a week then the children started to not like what he made. He would make them what they wanted for breakfast then send them off to school with lunch money. At night when he came home from work there was no dinner. I made dinner for myself which they could eat if they wanted. He made dinner for himself and the kids then, after a few dinners, the kids didn't like what he cooked. So the same thing was happening to him. He asked me if I would cook again. I said I would if he would give me some support. He reluctantly did.

The children came first to him. I was after the children. As a girlfriend said I was kind of his third child. I was there to do what he told me to do and to take care of his children. We were not a couple or a team; we were at opposite positions.

This time seemed to fly by and, before I knew it, both my children were in school full time. So the time came for me to go back to work. I had been going to school at night getting my master's in reading. I felt a reading teaching position was a good job for me. I also got my state certification as well as my city certification in elementary education and reading in New York. So now I was capable of getting a tenured teaching position in the city public schools and on Long Island.

My husband paid for my master's from Adelphi. So my stepfather and mother were right when they said let my husband pay for me to go to college. At least he paid for my master's from Adelphi. I had a free BA from Queens College.

I did go to my master's graduation from Adelphi. I still remember it. It was a beautiful sunny day. There were many graduates. I had a black cap and gown. My children, husband, and mother were there. It was a wonderful ceremony. I remember everyone really clapping for us and we threw little pieces of the program up in the air like confetti. After the ceremony we went to the Garden City Hotel and had a great brunch. It was just perfect. I enjoyed every minute of it.

My mother told me not to go back to work. To let my husband, pay the bills and worry about the money. I think in the back of my mind I knew I better go back to work and get some money so I would be able to support myself just in case.

Teaching positions were hard to come by on Long Island, at that time. I did get a part time reading position in Valley Stream. It was perfect. I was able to pick my children up from school at 3 o'clock and be home with them. I was off on Thursday, so I would pick them up from school for lunch and we would have our weekly fun lunch together.

My paycheck went right into our joint account and he had control of the money. Big mistake. In a marriage, you should both have your own accounts and a joint account but that is how stupid I was. I was working and didn't even have control of my money, a lower-class way of thinking.

My husband's businesses had been growing. He had three stores. Now they seemed to be getting into trouble. I felt probably because he gave many customers too much credit. He would have to go to court and confiscate some of his customers' property to get paid. Once he got a car and a boat. So for a time we owned a boat. Suddenly, my husband knew how to steer a boat. We did have some fun times on the boat. We would entertain friends and family. Everyone seemed to enjoy it. I did see how stupid people could be around water and boats.

One time, when we had my aunt and uncle on the boat, my uncle just dove in the water head first.

Never looking to see how the current was or how deep the water was. Luckily it was deep enough, but the current was very strong and we had to throw him a life preserver to get him back to the boat.

When it rained, my husband had to go to where the boat was docked to make sure it was OK. There was upkeep and rent. It was a wood boat. We only had it one season because on the way to the winter dock the boat sank. Yes, it sank. My husband, my four-year-old daughter, my brother-in-law and his ten-year-old son were on the boat when it hit a bridge, breaking the back of the boat. They didn't have life jackets on. Luckily, the Long Island Sound was as crowded as the Long Island Expressway and there were many boats around to rescue them. That was the end of the boat. It cost us much money to clean the boat out of the water. We lost money on that deal but at least everyone was safe.

Unfortunately, my part time position lasted three years then they laid all the part time reading teachers off. I took another part time reading position in Freeport. It seemed they wanted to keep these positions part time so they didn't have to give teachers tenure.

I serviced the Catholic school but was an employee of the Freeport school system. The Catholic school was entitled to a reading teacher and a nurse from the public school. It was funny because I wasn't allowed in the Catholic school. I had an assistant who walked the kids across the street to the library where my classroom was located.

Some Catholic schools had trailers outside the school so the reading teacher could take the students in there and service the Catholic school. It was strange the public-school employees weren't allowed in the Catholic school building. The nurse was allowed in because she needed to be there for the sick students. I went back to the building at lunchtime and had lunch with everyone. So it was a nice place to work.

In a few years, we needed money; so first, I asked Freeport if they would make my position full time. They said no. I went looking for a full time reading position and got one. It wasn't easy getting another position; I had to give a lesson in front of the principal and the superintendent but I got it. I gave my notice to Freeport. Surprisingly, they offered me a full time position if I stayed. Looking back, I was too quick to say I would stay. I should have negotiated tenure. This might sound great to you but it wasn't. I now know I should have gone to the other position. Freeport gave me no contract, saying they would keep me. I wasn't tenured. I stupidly didn't negotiate anything.

Unfortunately, the Catholic school closed the following year and they had to move me and the nurse to one of the public schools. They decided to make the Catholic school building into a public school. They renovated the building over the summer. They were supposed to have only tenured teachers in the new school but none of the other reading teachers wanted to go. So they asked me if I would take the position. I did. Another big mistake. If the reading teacher who the principal is working with didn't want to go with her and no other reading teacher wanted to work under her; that is a red flag. I should have realized something was going on. I was just happy I had a position in Freeport that was just made full time. I had always received good evaluations, so I felt pretty secure.

Well I got a rude awakening. The principal was a horror. She didn't like anything I did. Believe me, I tried to make her happy. At the end of the year, she had gotten rid of half the faculty, including me. The next year she got rid of the next reading teacher and finally the third year she kept the reading teacher, probably because that was the one she wanted in the first place.

I tried to keep that position. It was a lost cause. I just about had a nervous breakdown because I knew we needed the money and health insurance. Don't be fooled into thinking your employer is loyal to you. I don't think so. When they needed me, they made me full time to keep me. Now no administrators came to my rescue and put me into another school. Maybe they thought I wanted to leave anyway because I had told them I was leaving the year before. The union couldn't do much for me because I wasn't tenured. I should have negotiated that when they asked me to stay full time.

People at work are there for the job, not to make friends. It is a rude awakening how others avoid teachers the principal doesn't like. Teachers I had worked with for four years stayed away from me. I ate alone. The reading teachers didn't even say goodbye to me when I left.

When you lose a position, not only do you lose a salary, you lose health insurance too. Health insurance and your job should not be connected. You have enough to worry about with your salary gone, you shouldn't have to worry about health insurance, too. The health insurance they offer you when you lose your job is expensive. How are you going to pay it with no salary?

A few teachers from the Nassau Reading Council, where I had become a member, helped me get interviews in their school districts. I actually got offered three positions. I had begun to take help from my friends. I was beginning to understand I didn't have to do everything for myself. I could use my resources. My friends were my resources and they wanted to help. I was beginning to think and act as a middle-class person.

I didn't skip a beat. I got a job as a reading teacher for the New York City Board of Education in Queens. I remember going to the massive job interview. There must have been hundreds of people applying for positions. I even met some of the people I had worked with in Freeport. I almost left at first. I thought it was hopeless but I stayed and I got the job. It didn't pay as much, but I got really good health insurance and a great pension plan. When I started working, I was entitled to put ten percent of my salary into a TDA and they would match it. My husband didn't want me to do that. I had a big fight with him but I did it. I also got us long term health care against his advice.

I had seen my mother being sick for years. She didn't have long term health care. She was always afraid they would take her house if she had to go into a nursing home. Luckily that never happened. I knew you needed long term health care. My mother would stay with us after she had been in the hospital. She was constantly in and out of the hospital.

We were called the squeeze generation because we were being squeezed between our elderly parents and our children who needed us. There were many times I felt very squeezed trying to take care of my mother and my children.

My husband's businesses weren't doing well. In fact, he sold the business and didn't get much money for it. He then bought a hardware store. That didn't go well and soon he was looking for a job. He was now in his fifties and many men in their fifties find themselves having to change careers. Most people don't talk about it but many people get laid off or fired for whatever the reason and find themselves without a position in their fifties. This can be devastating for a man, especially. My husband found some jobs but it seemed every time Christmas rolled around he was out of work.

At some points, I was the only one working and we had my health insurance. My brother-in-law couldn't understand how we could have my health insurance. He was so narrow lower class minded he couldn't comprehend that a woman could be working and getting health insurance for the whole family.

I think, at that time, it was a threshold for women. Women just started to get equal pay for equal work. Most still had the mindset when a woman worked, it was not a serious job and the woman didn't really need it. Most felt women should depend on their husbands to bring in the money. Mostly, they felt women should stay with their husband and live off what he made. If you were a single woman then you were out of luck.

I came to the conclusion if you don't have to work, don't. Work is very stressful even if you find something you like. Uncontrollable things come into play, such as a principal you can't please or an impossible boss, whatever. If you could get a husband who had a good career and made much money, that was the way to go in my generation.

Now that I'm older, I meet many older women who have much money and most of them have it because they had a rich husband. They also probably came from a rich family and had good self-esteem to get the rich husband.

Chapter 25

My sister, at this point, had two children and lived in Boston. Her husband was a successful lawyer making money. She didn't work. She had a big house outside of Boston, a ski house in New Hampshire and a summer house in Maine. I went to visit her at her houses. The kids loved each other. They bonded and, to this day, they all have a good relationship.

There were times when my sister was snooty when I went to visit her. I remember one winter; we were all prepared to go to visit her at her ski house. She called me and told me she didn't want me to come. She felt my husband should be coming on some of these trips too. My husband rarely came to any of her houses. He was always working at his stores or wherever.

We were all packed. The kids were looking forward to it but we couldn't go. I took them ice skating and tried to make that week fun for them. It actually worked out—my kids learned how to ice skate and my son became a good ice hockey player.

When I went to her summer home in Maine, I met many snooty women who had many money. They wanted to know what my husband did so they could put me in the category they thought I belonged. Soon I just started to send my kids by themselves. My son John had wonderful summer visits with his cousins, Until this day he talks about it.

I realize now my sister was having her own problems in her marriage. She had a difficult husband she was trying to please. She was trying to fit in with the snooty women herself. She didn't tell anyone she was Italian. She didn't tell anyone about our absentee father. I guess me visiting wasn't helping her fit in.

I was also having problems in my marriage. My husband and I had different ideas about almost everything. I didn't agree with him about money and how it should be spent. I didn't agree with him about how the children should be raised. I didn't agree with him about where we should live and in what house. Our sex life was nil.

My husband's ideas about money were totally different from mine. His idea of paying the credit card bill was to pay the minimum. I totally disagreed with that. I wanted to pay in full and if we couldn't, we should stop spending.

I thought we should put money into the house. We should live in the best place we could afford. He disagreed. He didn't want to put money into the house. He was going to fix everything himself. He never was able to do that. We had a broken shower for fifteen years. He never finished what he started to fix in the house. When I hired someone, he told me I was wasting our money and we had a big fight.

He was also a hoarder. Our basement and garage were filled to the top with stuff. He never threw away anything. It was a constant battle to keep the main part of the house clean. He would start to put stuff in the dining room and I would take it and put it in the garage. He would get mad and we would have a fight.

I told him it's bad enough the basement and the garage is piled high with stuff but I wouldn't have the main house piled high with stuff too. Every day it was a constant battle, me taking his stuff out of the main house and putting it in the garage or basement. It is not easy living with a hoarder. They really have a disease.

The children were growing up and they were good kids. They never gave us any real problems. But my husband wanted to treat them as if they were royalty and I was the maid. They didn't have any real chores to do in the house. I remember one time we came home from a trip and we were all tired. They were twelve and fourteen at the time. He sent them into the house and expected me and him to unload the car. I saw no reason why they couldn't help us. He wanted them to just go and rest.

If they wanted a new computer, they were bought a new computer and I got the old one. I don't know if this is the way it should be or not. I just know how it made me feel. I felt to be a third child and not a wife and equal partner. Someone that was not special to him. The kids were number one in my husband's life.

I remember when we went to visit Susanne at Holy Cross and we were all going out to dinner. Her boyfriend was with us and we had two cars. The cars were parked in different directions so we all left to get into the cars. I ran behind my husband in hopes I would be able to keep up with him but I wasn't. They all left without me. I don't remember if we had cell phones in those days but when they got to the restaurant they realized I wasn't in any of the cars. They came back for me but I just felt this is how important I was to my husband. He didn't seem sorry in fact he seemed annoyed as if it were my fault I didn't get into the cars.

Another time I had gone to a school dinner and one of the teachers drove me. She had been drinking rather heavily so I didn't want to ride home with her. I called and asked my husband if he could come and get me. I had to call three times before he finally left. The house was about fifteen minutes away; it's not as if I were asking him to drive a distance. When he got there he was mad and said I should have taken a taxi. The taxi stand was just a little bit away. Maybe I was overly sensitive but this made me feel as if he really didn't care much about me.

I wanted to move to a bigger house. He didn't. I was working and his business seemed to be doing well at that time. My best girlfriend moved to Rockville Centre to a big house. My dream was to have a big kitchen before I died. For years, I went looking at houses. We didn't fix up the house because he said we would move. We put down payments on houses and then bailed out.

After a few years, I felt he was just patting me on the head and making a fool of me. We had a big fight and, finally, bought a house in Rockville Centre with a big kitchen. It was a center hall colonial, with a pool in the backyard. It was the nicest house I ever owned. He acted as if I made him move to hell. He made the kids feel they were moving to the worst place in the world. If something went wrong, the kids would say it's because you made us move here.

I felt as if he wanted to beat me down and make me regret wanting to move. The more I tried the more I was told how horrible the move was. His sister told me her brother could have died because of the move. It was a horrible first few years in the house.

My mother even said she didn't understand the way he and the kids acted. We moved to a bigger and nicer house. They acted as if we had moved to a hellhole. I felt alone and I felt the three of them were against me. I couldn't please them no matter what I did. I was the horrible person who dared to want a bigger house and go against my husband's wishes.

I guess, in his eyes, the wife should obey the husband. He was the boss and how dare I want something he didn't approve of or want a lower-class idea also an idea that didn't work for having a good marriage. If partners support the other one's wants and learn to try to compromise and give, then you have a good marriage.

Years went by and I felt numb, going through the motions. One time, we went to a gathering and I realized I was old and frumpy. I had gotten into a rut. Just doing what I had to do, not getting much joy and not really paying attention to how I was starting to look. I had gained about twenty pounds.

We were not partners anymore. We both stopped caring about each other's dreams a long time ago. We didn't support each other and we didn't have respect for one another. I had changed and I wasn't the obedient Italian girl he married. I had become a middle-class wife with middle-class ideas, which didn't work in the lower-class marriage, such as mine.

We started going to counseling after he pushed me. We addressed the money problem, never really solving it. We addressed the children's situation and agreed to come to some compromise in parenting them. That was very strained. We agreed to some time limit on his fixing things in the house then I could hire someone. We never really fixed our sexual problem. He said I was frigid. I said he was impotent.

I remember one time; the counselor asked me what number I felt I was in my husband's life. I said number six. My husband said no, I was number one but I felt I was number six. The two kids came first then his two aunts then his uncle and last, me.

I remember my sister saying her husband once set up the answering machine and it said press one for Roger, press two for Carrie, press three for George and press four for Francine. That said it all. She was number four.

One thing I know for sure, if you and your husband are not number one to each other then the marriage is doomed. You are not going to be able to take care of the kids or anything else. You have to take care of your relationship first.

Marriage is akin to a big boulder. When you first get married you are hopefully in a big solid boulder of a relationship. Then slowly life starts chipping away at the boulder. Until you stop the chipping or until there is nothing left. That's the way your relationship goes. Either it stays a strong boulder or it becomes chipped away to nothing.

Also there is never one person who is right and one person who is wrong in a divorce. The ones involved are both right and wrong. After a divorce, I wouldn't say the marriage is a failure. Some good comes out of everything. I had two beautiful children. I grew as a person. I learned much about myself. I learned who my true friends were. Your true friends help you during a divorce whether they think you are right or wrong. I learned how important and helpful family was, especially at that time.

Chapter 26

I was unhappy for a long time. The kids were now twenty-three and twenty-one and they were both out of the house. My mother had died the year before. My husband and I really weren't company for each other. We didn't go out as a couple anymore. I used to go out with a girlfriend every Friday night to dinner.

One of the last times my husband and I went out as a couple was with his best man, his wife and my sister. We were supposed to go out for dinner. We had made the plan weeks ago. My husband didn't want to go because he was waiting for a call from our daughter. He wanted to pick her up at the airport. He had a cell phone but that wasn't good enough.

He acted as if he didn't even want to go out with any of us. Although we'd planned to go out with them, he still he didn't want to do anything. Our best man, at one point told my husband go and stand by your bride, maybe trying to tell him he had a wife. Finally, when my daughter called, he left to go get her, leaving us all at the house. My sister said if she didn't know better she would have thought he didn't like his best man and his wife because he didn't want to do anything. She didn't mention that it looked like he didn't want to go out with me either.

His children were number one. He didn't care about having a relationship with me or even his friends. There were many of those evenings. So, I just started going out with my girlfriends by myself. I wanted out of the marriage but didn't know how to go about it. I guess I was just going through the motions because I was used to my life even if I was unhappy.

One day I got an email from an old boyfriend. He had found my email because I had written a book and used my maiden name. I wrote a book after I was fired from Freeport; mostly to express my feelings. It turned out to be a self-help book on how to be a teacher. It was titled *So You Want to Be a Teacher* (Frederick Fell's Official Know-it-All-Guide).

The old boyfriend wanted to know if I was the same person he went out with almost thirty years ago. I was. He was the guy who treated me special but had the two children and didn't want any more children. We started emailing.

I finally started to feel special again. We emailed every day, sometimes many times a day. It was my escape from my humdrum life. I started to lose weight. I started to want to do things for myself again. At this point, I didn't feel married. I felt alone as if I were single. My marriage wasn't what I called a marriage anymore. We never went out together. We just went through the motions. It was as if I were living with an acquaintance. It had been that way for ten years, just living like brother and sister. I once read that sex is about fifty percent of the marriage but, if there is no sex it becomes a hundred percent of the marriage. Knowing that we would never have sex again became a big issue in my marriage.

I would envy people who were divorced or single because they at least had hope of happiness—I was numb with unhappiness. Those years were the years I want to forget because I can't believe I stayed so unhappy for so long and did nothing about it. I emailed my old boyfriend for months. Finally, we decided we would meet in Florida. I felt alive again with anticipation; I wanted some joy in my life. So, I made an excuse to my husband I was going to Florida to meet my publisher. I don't think he even cared or missed me.

I didn't feel as if I were doing anything wrong because I didn't feel I was married anymore. I didn't even try to hide the emails I was writing to him. A girlfriend told me to not let anyone know and get a divorce then, in six months or so, after the divorce, tell people I met an old boyfriend. I should have done that but I really didn't feel I wasn't doing anything wrong. I did meet him in Florida. It was wonderful, just like old times. He treated me so special. I hadn't felt special in years. It was a glorious weekend. We planned to meet in California, where he lived, in a few weeks. When I got back to New York I decided I would get a divorce. I decided to wait and proceed after I came back from California.

Unfortunately, when I was in California my husband found my emails to him. He told my children and his family. He acted as if I were his property and how dare I do such a thing to him and the family. By the time I got back to New York, everyone knew from him what I had done. I stayed with my girlfriend.

When he calmed down I went back to the house. It was a living a nightmare. I was afraid of him. I really didn't think he cared about me and our relationship. It was more about his property being a disgrace to him. I felt he really thought he owned me and I was supposed to obey him and do what he wanted, no matter what. He wanted to go to counseling. I said no, I wanted a divorce. My daughter came to talk to me. I wasn't changing my mind. The wheels had started to turn. I wanted out. I couldn't go back to being so miserable. Even if it didn't work out with the old boyfriend, I wanted out of the marriage.

My son stopped talking to me. I was shocked at their responses to the situation. I realize they thought everything had been fine or they didn't want to know everything wasn't fine. They had no idea I was so unhappy for such a long time; to them, nothing was wrong. They didn't want their parents to break up. I was the bad guy, their father was wonderful and what was wrong with me. It was true their father was wonderful. A wonderful father, not a wonderful husband. Many people were shocked, actually, most people were shocked.

I still was surprised people were acting as if I had done something wrong. I felt I had taken control of my life and made myself happy. My husband got worse. He threatened to give me a good beating. He started saying he wanted the divorce and he was divorcing me. We both got lawyers. That is when I went to live with my best friend. This was a major inconvenience for her, but I really needed to stay with someone. I had no money. All my money had gone into the joint account that now had nothing in it. The only money I had was six thousand dollars that was in a joint account my mother and I had. Now that she was dead, it was all I had.

I decided to retire from my job at the NYC Board of Education in June and go to California. I was fifty-five and able to retire. It was only April and I had to stay somewhere. I stayed with my girlfriend most of the time. She was my life saver. I was afraid of my husband so I couldn't go home. I had only six thousand dollars so I didn't have money to stay in a hotel. My sister lived in Boston so I couldn't go to her. I needed to stay in New York until June.

My girlfriend was wonderful but she did want me to go back to my husband. Even my cousin told me to go back to my husband if I could. My girlfriend's ninety-year-old mother told me if I'm strong enough to leave him then it's the right thing to do. The older women seemed to understand what I was going through and what I felt. Another older woman wished me good luck and hoped everything worked out.

The main reason I was comfortable divorcing him was I knew I could take care of myself. I had a career. I could get a teaching job and earn my own living. I was now a middle-class woman. Lower-class women usually can't take care of themselves financially, so they stay in unhappy marriages. Even though I knew I could take care of myself financially, I was a nervous wreck. I could hardly function. My sister came down to help me. She rented an apartment in Manhattan for a month and I stayed with her. She seemed to help me and support me. People at work suspected something was wrong but I didn't say too much. Somehow I got through until June. The school gave the retirees a party. I went and the teachers did a cute skit in my favor. The party was fun. Afterward, I met my sister and we went to a Cher concert in Manhattan.

My son wasn't talking to me; my daughter just barely spoke to me; so my retirement was not a family affair. My sister was as supportive as she could be. She never told me I was doing anything wrong. She had been divorced for a few years now. Her children were barely talking to her either because she divorced their "wonderful" father.

Chapter 27

My girlfriend drove me to the airport and told me I was ruining my life but I got on the plane anyway and went to California. My old boyfriend was there waiting for me at the airport. He was so happy to see me. He adored me; he couldn't do enough for me. I was going to try to get my own apartment but we decided I would stay with him. I loved it. He treated me with respect and so special I couldn't believe my good fortune. If I was in my twenties and had no children or responsibilities back in New York, it would have been perfect. I tried keeping up with my children. I called and emailed them.

When Thanksgiving came, I flew back to Boston to have Thanksgiving at my sister's place where my daughter and niece would be. I was so glad to see my family, especially my daughter. She was quick to cry and made me feel as if I'd done the most horrible thing to her. I felt so guilty but, at this point, it was done and there was no going back. It was as if I had jumped off a cliff and while falling started to make a parachute. Everyone had to adjust. Everyone was used to the way things used to be; I was the culprit who changed everything. My family and friends were used to me doing certain things. I would give big Fourth of July parties and I had Easter. That didn't happen this year.

I was beginning to realize I just didn't leave my husband. I left New York where my family and friends were. If I could have stayed in New York it would have been an easier divorce. The most difficult thing for me was leaving my family and friends; especially my children, who were now about twenty-one and twenty-three.

When I went to visit, it was wonderful being back in the East. California was beautiful, especially the weather, but it was a lot different from the East. He lived in Milpitas, a town not far from San Francisco. Everyone and everything was laid back and easy going in California. Signs on the stores would say be back soon. Not be back at a certain time. Plants would grow differently. In the East, first leaves would grow then the flowers. In California I saw flowers grow first then the leaves. It was definitely different.

Memories

There were many young people in California. Everything was young there. It was a young territory. It seemed the history there started during the gold rush in the 1840's not as in the East where the history started in the 1700's. The few friends he had were much younger than we were. Most of them were IT people who made good money. His friends didn't have many family members there. It seemed friends were family to each other out there. Some of his friends were orphans. I felt a little old being around them even though they were friendly. Even where I worked, I was the oldest.

I had found a part time reading teacher position there and was making a little money. My pension had started but it wasn't very much. I found it easy to get a position in California, mostly because I was a New Yorker. Even though I was an older woman they still wanted to hire me. I started volunteering at the local hospital because I started to write my second book, *So You Want to Be a Nurse* and needed to get some information about nurses in a hospital.

I joined a church and met many friendly people. Most of them didn't have much family in California either. I would say most people had moved there, away from family, maybe because of the weather, maybe because of the IT work there. For the first time in my life I was away from family. I was starting to feel the results of moving there. The people of the church were supportive. Even though my boyfriend, who I was now living with was very good to me, I missed my family and friends.

I had painted many pictures about 9/11 and now had them in California. The local library had agreed to have a showing of my paintings and memorabilia during the month of September. After the showing, there would be a small reception. Everyone from the church showed up. Even some of the nurses from the hospital showed up. I was so happy to see them. I was afraid I wouldn't have anyone there.

The 9/11 event was a horrible thing that happened in New York. I was working at a school in Queens. Someone had a radio and the word got out what had happened. We also could see the twin towers with all the smoke from the classroom windows. They started calling all the parents so they could come and get their children. They put mats down on the gym floors just in case we had to stay the night.

Luckily we were all able to go home. The parkway was blocked off going into the city. There were no cars on the west side of the parkway. Then you would go a few exits and see the whole mass of cars just stopped and not allowed to go any further. Luckily I was going east on the parkway and got home. I never saw anything to equal that in my life. There were no planes in the sky, only a helicopter flying around occasionally.

When I got home, my daughter in Manhattan called and told us she was all right. She had walked to a friend's apartment and was safe there but an English friend of hers couldn't call his parents in London to tell them he was OK. So I tried and was able to get through. I got someone who knew his parents and would tell them he was all right. The person also said how sorry he was about what had happened and all of England was sorry and wished us well. The phones were working sporadically. We finally were able to call my son in Ireland and told him we were all OK.

Friends of ours lost relatives and wives and husbands. Thank God no one close to us died. We heard horror stories. Everyone was somewhat afraid but yet strong. No one wanted to go into the city. The police and firemen became heroes. People wanted to shake their hands. Mayor Giuliani was a hero too. He never slept; he tried to go to every funeral and help in any way he could. He was a great leader at that time. I didn't like him before 9/11 but I certainly respected him after.

So I had painted some paintings to try to elevate some of the horrible feelings of 9/11. I had taken them with me to California. Nine/eleven was still on everyone's mind at the time and the local library was interested in displaying them. So I was settling in, living in California.

I was finding it very hard being away from New York and my family and friends. Even though my boyfriend was supportive, I finally had to go to a psychologist who put me on some medication to calm my anxiety. I started to feel better.

I went back to New York as often as possible that first year. Every holiday I was in New York or Boston. My sister's house now was my base house when I flew back east. In six months, my son started to talk to me. That year my daughter was accepted into San Diego Law School. I started going down to San Diego to help her find an apartment and get her settled.

My sister came out to California a few times. One time, my sister, my daughter, niece and I were all in San Diego at the same time. We had a wonderful visit going down to Mexico and to the San Diego zoo. It was great. My son, John, even came to San Diego and we went to Mexico. My girlfriend stopped in California on her way to Hawaii, so I saw her and her two boys. We even looked up a cousin in San Francisco and had dinner with him a few times. It was slowly working out, but it was a very trying year with family and friends. Most of the time, even though my children were talking to me, it was strained and they hinted how horrible it had been for them. Some of my family members hinted they missed the way it used to be.

The first Christmas I went back to New York, I cried the whole Christmas Eve at my cousin's house. We had been having Christmas Eve at my cousin's house in Connecticut for a few years now, ever since my aunt died. They were wonderful New England Christmases and we always enjoyed them. Now I was there without my children. I was nervous, it was awful. My family tried to console me. My uncle said, I'm glad my sister isn't alive to see this. It was the worst Christmas of my life. It just was an enormous, stressful change for me. My children spent Christmas with their father. That started a trend, every holiday they spent with him. I was the outcast.

They didn't want to alternate holidays; they wanted to be with him. For years they spent holidays with him and I was on my own. I would go to my sister and cousin's Christmas on my own. I was lonely and wanted to be around my family more. My boyfriend was Jewish, so he didn't care if I was away on Christmas. I always returned for New Year's and we went out then.

Chapter 28

I guess you could say this was my change of life stage. Someone who gets a divorce, moves to a different state and lives with an old boyfriend is going through a life change. At first, I was very nervous about living with my old boyfriend but after sometime I knew I could trust him and he always treated me with respect. When he said he was going to pick me up, he always was on time. He took me out and we explored various sights in California. We went to Bonanza TV studio, to Reno and the Gold rush tourist spots. He was OK with me going to New York often. At that time, he was supportive to me and wanted the best for me.

He asked me to marry him, and I said yes. Our life together was wonderful. We had our moments the same way as every other couple but despite that, we were always happy. He treated me with respect and I am certain I was his first priority in life. We seemed to agree on the three basic things for a good marriage: family, money and sex.

He was a smoker and I had to get used to that, a terrible habit. This came as a shock to me because he was very detail-oriented and neat; a pleasant change from the hoarder with whom I had lived. I had to get used to putting things back exactly where I had removed them. At the end of the day, I knew I had made the right decision by marrying him.

We decided we would live in Florida as California was too expensive for two retirees. He had retired a decade ago. There were many reasons why Florida was the ideal place for us to live. One, his parents lived in Florida and this meant we would be neighbors. Second, the time zone in New York and Florida was the same, making it easy to fly to New York. Lastly, I loved Florida. I fell in love with the place when I went for a vacation. The weather is beautiful, the streets are clean and the people there are friendly. So, we put both houses up for sale. My house in Rockville Centre and my mother's house in Ozone Park, which my sister and I owned was for sale, not forgetting my divorce was proceeding.

Divorce is usually a messy affair. I don't think many people have friendly divorces. If you can stay married then do so. If you can't and realize you must hire lawyers then get the best lawyer you can and get out of the legal system as quickly as possible. The longer you stay in the legal system, the more money you lose. You may fight for ten thousand dollars and spend fifteen thousand trying to get it. Just settle as fast as you can even if you think you are getting an unfair deal. The quicker you settle and get the divorce the more you gain. The emotional toll is enough to make you want it to stop as soon as possible. Just get on with your life, don't let it drag out for a few thousand dollars. It isn't worth it. Just get out of the legal system as soon as possible. This refers to anything in the legal system, not just divorces. This is what I did. I got the divorce as soon as possible. I know I got a bad deal. I didn't even get half the house but at least I didn't have thousands and thousands of lawyer bills.

Soon we started getting offers for the houses we had put up for sale. I flew back for the house closing in Rockville Centre, and I had to see my husband at the closing. It was very difficult. Just one of those things you had to do and get done. Then my mother's house sold. My sister took care of that closing. Finally, my fiancé's house closed and we were on our way. We could finally relocate to Florida. Now, looking back, I don't know how all those changes took place that year, but they did. I must admit, I was a nervous wreck that year. One minute I was guilty, the next elated. It was a frightening, anxiety-filled but an exciting year for me. I was just relieved the whole thing got settled fast.

Chapter 29

So we settled in Florida. With the money we both had from the sale of our houses, we soon bought a little house in Wellington. We had no mortgage. I also eventually bought two condos for income property in Davie, no mortgages.

The first summer, immediately after the wedding, we went to New York to get the things I had in storage. I also introduced my new husband to my family and friends who hadn't been at the wedding. Then we drove back to Florida with my things in a U-Haul. On the way down, we saw a massive amount of cars going north. We heard a hurricane was going to hit Florida, and people were leaving. We continued to drive down. When we got to our house, we had a few days until the hurricane was going to hit. I had never been in a hurricane so I had no idea what to do. We had to board up all the windows with big plywood boards that the old owners had left in the garage. We had to screw them in. The next door neighbor came over and helped us. Then we had to get prepared for no electricity, get gas in the cars, get food that didn't have to be refrigerated, and water. Everything had to be taken in from outside, including the water hose, lawn furniture, flower pots, everything.

When the hurricane hit, we had to stay in the middle of the house where there were no windows, which was a walk-in closet in the main bedroom. We all but slept there during the night. We heard the hurricane but couldn't see anything for everything was boarded up. It was scary.

The next morning when the hurricane had passed we ventured outside. There was garbage everywhere. Shingles from roofs had blown off and hit houses and stuck out like knives. Trees had fallen. One tree had fallen on a neighbor's car. Luckily, we had put our two cars in the garage. The front lawn was covered with branches, leaves, sticks, and parts of people's houses.

No one had electricity and, because it was August, it was hot. We started cleaning up the front lawn. People started barbecuing the food from their refrigerators. Neighbors were all outside. Inside was too hot, especially because all the windows were boarded up. One thing good about hurricanes is you get to know your neighbors. The airports were closed, so were all the stores and most of the gas stations.

We were lucky, in three days we had our electricity back. We were on the same electrical grid as the police station, so we got our electricity back as soon as possible. Some of our friends had no electricity for weeks. Some of them came over to my house to use the shower. Yes, there is no hot water when you have no electricity. Another hurricane was predicted to hit in about a week, so we didn't take down the boards until after that one. We lived in what felt to be a cave. They said Florida hadn't had a hurricane in twenty years and that year it got two major ones.

I've been in Florida sixteen years now and there have been a few hurricanes. Luckily, you get a few days' warning so you can decide if you want to stay or not. The one time we evacuated was worse than if we had stayed. We drove eighteen hours to Atlanta, which was horrendous and the hurricane did not hit our area too hard. A tree did fall on my car but I was able to get it fixed. Anywhere you live has something. We soon learned to live with hurricanes. We hoped they wouldn't hit but, if they did we had a few days to prepare. That first summer things did go back to normal after the hurricane. We settled into our new home and I started to evaluate what I had to do.

I knew I had to work until I could collect Social Security. My New York pension wasn't enough to live well. I wanted to work part time and I quickly got a part time job as a Special Education teacher in the Palm Beach County School District. I found, to my pleasure, they needed teachers, especially certified teachers. Even though I was an older woman, now fifty-six, I was able to get a position.

I started working and because I was older it took a toll on me. I was tired. I liked part time work because I had a day off. In a few years they insisted I go in the classroom as a full time teacher. They were having trouble getting teachers. What a surprise— they didn't pay well and they had done away with tenure. Most of the administrators took the parents' side over the teacher. No one seemed to respect teachers. They were hiring people who had never taken an education course to teach, and expected the experienced teachers to train them, with no extra pay. I just stuck it out because, as soon as I was sixty-six, I was going to retire. That is what I did. With Florida and New York City pensions, plus Social Security and my two income properties, I would be able to have a good retirement.

I had joined the Episcopalian church and the Wellington Women's club. I wanted to meet people and make friends. We did. I met many friends from church and from the Wellington Women's club. When I joined the Wellington Women's club, there must have been two hundred members. They had all sorts of activities. I then joined the Red Hatters through the Women's club. So I was starting to do things and make friends. I still was lonely for my family and friends. In about a year or so, my daughter told me the good news. She and her husband were looking to find positions in Florida. They both were lawyers in Washington D.C. The Washington law firms weren't doing well. So my daughter and her husband were looking for positions in Florida. I was overjoyed. It took a few years but they were both down in Florida and working as lawyers.

During those first few years, many people visited us in Florida. My sister came and so did my sister-in-law and her husband. My sister was going to buy a place the first year we were in Florida but that summer the hurricanes came and no one was buying anything in Florida for a while. Then, in a few years, she started to rent her own place and stayed for a few months.

My sister-in-law bought a house near us in Florida in a few years. Then my sister rented an apartment all year in Florida right by us. So in a few years I had my daughter, her husband, my sister, and sister-in-law and her husband living right near us. I was ecstatic.

My husband enjoyed going to charity balls. He bought us a membership to the Palm Beach Symphony and in season we went to the symphony at places, such as Mar-a-Lago and The Breakers. Then, after the symphony, we went to exquisite restaurants in Palm Beach with the symphony group.

The women had high teas every year at one of the exquisite restaurants in Palm Beach. They usually had opera singers for entertainment and a raffle where one ticket was twenty-five dollars. It was wonderful. I loved it.

He also bought us tickets to go to big charity balls in Palm Beach. We would start the season off going to The Lady in Red at Mar-a-Lago. It was the most extravagant ball I ever attended. Nothing could compare to the Lady in Red at Mar-a-Lago. It was beyond being with the higher class rich. The first year we went I met Donald Trump and Jay Leno. I have a picture with them. We went to The Lady in Red for at least six years. We stopped going when they moved it to The Breakers. My sister even started going with us.

My husband loved New Year's Eve so he booked us tickets to The Fantasy Ball at The Breakers on New Year's Eve. I don't know if there is any place on earth that can compare to The Breakers on New Year's Eve. Maybe a few; including Mar-a-Lago but The Breakers was definitely where the rich and famous went on New Year's Eve.

You name it, you got it, at The Breakers—wonderful cocktail hour with entertainment. Anything you could imagine was there to eat. The dinner never ended. The band was wonderful. You couldn't eat or drink all that they gave you. It was the most wonderful New Year's Eves I ever spent. We went there at least four times. Once my sister went too. We started going out with a few couples and they didn't want to go to the Breakers for New Year's, so we started going to other places.

The best ball I ever went to was the Red Cross Ball at Mar-a-Lago. They had royalty everywhere—princes, princesses, counts, countesses, politicians and dignitaries. They were all announced and marched in when the ball began. I never thought I would be at a ball with these aristocratic people. Plus, I didn't feel intimidated. I was talking to them and felt as if I fit in.

By this time, I had been initiated into the wealthy by going to the Palm Beach symphony and now felt comfortable talking to the wealthy. I came to terms with them being just people who wanted to be friendly and make conversation. At these places, people just assumed you had money or you wouldn't be there.

I was the one, who, at first was being a snob at the dinners the Palm Beach Symphony gave. I wasn't talking to these rich people because I was afraid they wouldn't accept me yet no one talked about how much money they had. Maybe once in a while, someone dropped words such as my yacht or my plane but it wasn't to brag.

Remember the saying, "No one is too rich that they cannot receive, and no one is too poor that they cannot give." I finally came to terms with that saying. They were just people; some I would like and become friends with, others I wouldn't. Just as with any group of people you meet.

I now have some very wealthy friends; they are probably millionaires. They are my friends the same as my middle-class and lower-class ones. They still like someone to call them and ask how they are. They still want to be included in the group. You just have to find the person you click with as a friend, no matter what their social status is.

Whether you're rich or poor, black or white, male or female, everyone has some kind of problems. No one has a perfect life. There is a story about a group of people who sat around a table and listened to each other's problems. They can exchange problems if they want but, in the end, they all took their own problem back. It is a matter of mind getting out of poverty. You have to be willing to change and acknowledge maybe the ways you were taught are not the only ways. You have to pick which people are going to help you and push you up. You have to be willing to listen to strangers and learn from them. Also, it's hard work, getting an education definitely helps; being married to the right person also helps. A little bit of luck also helps. You have to be willing to take chances and change your life. You have to want to do it.

Time went on and it seemed as if everything were falling into place. My daughter, her husband and their two children now lived about an hour away. I went to visit them every week. My sister lived in Florida in season, so I saw her often. My sister-in-law and her husband came down in January and stayed until April. My son still didn't accept my husband but I saw him a few times a year. Either I went up to New York or he came down to Florida and stayed with his sister. He now had a wife and son. I even went to Italy with him one summer.

We had fairly enjoyable holidays. At first, my children would only spend the holidays with my ex-husband. As years went by, they spent some holidays with me, especially my daughter who was in Florida.

Memories

The holidays weren't as wonderful as when I was young and with the whole family, especially Christmas Eve, but they were enjoyable. We started making new traditions. Now we had all of Palm Beach splendor to use. I eventually stopped going to New York for holidays. The weather was too trying. One time, my plane was cancelled because of a snow storm. I drove back to Florida with a girlfriend. It was not fun.

I went on a couple of trips to Europe with my girlfriends. My husband was not well enough to travel. He had a triple bypass and COPD. So I went to Europe with my girlfriends. The best trip I went on was the cruise to Russia. We took a plane to Copenhagen then got on the cruise ship and went to Germany, Estonia, Russia, England, Ireland and Scotland. It was wonderful. It was the trip of my dreams and I can honestly say I've been everywhere I really wanted to go.

Chapter 30

Now I'm seventy-two years old and self-quarantining in my Florida house because of the COVID virus. I'm wondering what is happening in the world. I never experienced anything close to this. Why are so many people dying around the world? Why was everyone's life disrupted? My life was disrupted. I haven't gone anywhere in months. Everything is closed and there is nowhere to go. You can't travel to be near family. You have to stay put. So everyone is home, hoping their life will return.

I appreciated my life. I had my daughter near me. I visited her once a week and saw my two grandchildren. I haven't seen them in months. I would go to New York and see my son as much as I could. I can't do that anymore, either.

I would go to church every week and worship and socialize. Churches are closed. I watched Sunday mass on video. Daughters of the King of which I am a member, have zoom meetings instead of in-person meetings. I miss seeing people live.

My book club and Alpha Delta Kappa clubs were held on zoom. I actually hosted the zoom meetings. It was starting to feel as if we weren't connected. They stopped for the summer anyway. Are they ever going to resume?

Our croquet club was closed. We had a small group zoom meeting going. I miss making cakes for the croquet club members who had birthdays that month. That was one of my hobbies, making cakes. I love baking cakes for the croquet club. Now that was gone, too. We socialized through the croquet club…dinners, dances, Fourth of July, Memorial Day barbeques, Easter Sunday brunch, all stopped.

Even the way we celebrated birthdays, retirements and anniversaries changed. Drive-thru started. People would drive past the person's house, or wherever, at a certain time and they would be out front and they would congratulate them.

We did this for our pastor for his anniversary. We all drove by the parking lot of the church when he was there and wished him a happy anniversary. They were doing it for kids' graduation, birthdays you name it, that's what they did.

Actually in one way, it was better than having a typical party. I went to a drive thru party for a retiring teacher. Typically, they would give you a party during one of the teacher's work days and you would just have the faculty there. With the drive thru, everyone was there. All her students from the past years drove by with their parents in their cars, all her friends and family and the entire faculty. There were many cars in the line driving past and congratulating her. You could even give her a little something through the car window.

Even my Kravis Center volunteering stopped. No more live shows in the theaters. I would usher in at least twenty shows in a season and see all of them for free. I saw Hamilton three times for free. Actually, I wasn't that impressed with it but I was glad to see what all the hoopla was about.

I loved ushering the ballet and opera. I used to pay much money for season tickets to see them. Not only was I seeing the shows I wanted to see, I was seeing shows I never thought to see. I also got free tickets to shows that didn't sell out. So, overall, I loved ushering at the Kravis center. Now that is closed. Who knows when it will open? Look at Broadway. I never thought they would close Broadway.

I had a pleasant retirement life. I was social, had enough money to pay my bills and then some. Now I force myself to walk, to not get depressed about my lost life and all the death from the virus. I walk in the morning for a half hour and at night for a half hour. I wondered what I was going to do when it really got hot. At least the walks now kept me from getting too depressed. I was eating more carbs, probably gaining more weight than I wanted.

Some good was coming out of the virus quarantine, though. Families were instantly forced to be home with each other. Parents now had to teach their children, work from home and keep the house running. There were no more babysitters taking care of the children, all day long. No more afterschool to take care of the children until 6 o'clock in the evening. Families were getting to know each other and evaluating things. I also think this made people reevaluate their lives and see how they wanted to continue.

Parents were forced to teach their children. The video schooling couldn't do it all. They found out very quickly teaching their child wasn't so easy. Maybe it wasn't always the teacher's fault. They started respecting teachers again. Parents started asking anyone they knew who was a teacher, to help them teach their child. Grandma, who was a retired teacher, became very useful and needed. I started teaching reading to my granddaughter and my niece's son, over zoom.

People also started to evaluate their work habits. Maybe working from 8 o'clock in the morning until 6, 7 or 8 o'clock at night wasn't such a good thing. They started to realize they were missing their children's childhood. The old values of being home with your children were coming back. So people were evaluating their lives.

Some decided to change it dramatically. That's what I think my daughter did. She decided to go to Canada so they wouldn't have to work long hours. She would be home when the kids got home from school. Maybe she could enjoy her children's childhood. I still don't understand why she couldn't do that in the US but it was not my decision to make. I have no control over what they decide to do with their lives. Her husband was from Canada. Canada seemed to have the virus under control better than the United States. They had his family in Canada to live near.

My son went to Poland, where his wife came from, to ride out the Pandemic. They said Poland and Europe were open, and doing fine, compared to the United States. They decided to go to the Netherlands and put their son in a private school that was open, as it was before the pandemic.

Some people were forced to change their lives. Their jobs disappeared. They had to do something else. In the meantime, they were home with the children all day. Maybe for the first time since the children were born. They had to re-evaluate everything because now there was only one salary. Maybe the big house that the two of them worked for wasn't such a good idea. There were also the unfortunate ones, where both people lost their jobs. Or maybe the single parent lost their job. These were the ones just hanging on before the virus, now they had fallen. They needed every bit of help they could get.

We were fortunate. Everyone in my family, including myself, had enough money to live. My tenants were able to pay me the rent on my two income properties. My two pensions and social security were still coming. So my finances didn't change. Everyone got a severance check. I actually found myself saving money. I wasn't going out to dinner or movies. I wasn't spending money at the croquet club. I wasn't getting my hair done. I wasn't traveling down to Miami. I wasn't buying any toys or clothes. I wasn't buying gas. I wasn't buying or doing anything.

I guess many people weren't spending much money. That's why so many businesses were in trouble. Businesses were closing, especially restaurants and theaters. They started to reinvent the restaurant to include only take out and deliveries. The Kravis Center started streaming shows. I don't know if they were successful with that.

I eventually started buying things, mostly online. I now found I had money to buy things I normally wouldn't buy, especially things for myself. I ordered everything online, never went to a store. Because we were home, many things for the house became important. Things we could buy and not have to have a man come in and install. Home Depot and Lowes, stores such as that, were doing great. People were fixing up their homes.

Also, the living conditions changed. The trend had been for young families to live in apartments. The parents worked long hours and didn't want to come home and fix a house, on the weekend. So, they moved to a condominium, where they had all the amenities. Now that everyone was home, these apartments became too crowded. Also the big buildings had a greater chance of spreading the virus—elevators, lobbies, everyone in one building. Not as safe as a single house. So, many families wanted to move to houses. Some older people, found the house too lonely, and were having trouble keeping it up. No one wanted to hire people to come into their house and work—more chance of getting the virus. So these people wanted to move to apartments, where everything was done for them. So there was a great change in the living situation.

We didn't want to change our one family house. Luckily, we could still keep it up but my two children wanted to move. They were both living in apartments but now they wanted to live in houses and leave the country. They both had rented houses at the beginning of the virus. My son rented a house in Maine, just to get out of New York. My daughter rented a house outside of Miami, just to be safer.

Things started changing. People were afraid to go to stores. They wore masks and gloves. Food delivery became very popular. That's what we did. We had our food delivered. When it arrived, we washed every item down with Clorox. Internet sales ski rocked. I bought everything over the internet, mostly from Amazon Prime. Everyone was afraid of getting sick. Not only of contracting the virus but other things, too. Nobody wanted to go to the doctor or especially the emergency room. The doctors were doing virtual appointments. You couldn't get to see a live doctor. All those who had the virus were going to the emergency room. The ERs were overwhelmed.

I guess people felt I'm not dying then I'm all right and I'll take my chances over the emergency room where I can catch the virus. Most elective surgeries were canceled. Only necessary surgeries were done.

God help you, if you got the virus, especially in the beginning. Mostly older people were dying from the virus then. They really didn't have any medication or treatment they knew would work. The worst was when they put you in a coma to put you on ventilator. You had a very small chance of surviving that. It was horrible, and extremely scary.

People were told to wear masks, gloves, stay six feet apart and wash their hands frequently. The older people obeyed. The younger people, however, thought they were above it all. The virus didn't affect them. Well later, the young started dying of it too. So it became everyone's disease. Thankfully, it wasn't a virus that did much harm to children. For the most part, the children were safe.

I had a cardiac ablation on March ninth, right before the virus hit Florida. The virus was just talk then. I was glad I had the ablation done. I was going to wait and have it at the end of March. Luckily, the cardiologist had a cancellation and was able to treat my case. I was used to going to my daughter's on Monday and really didn't want to miss our visit. I was feeling so awful with my AFIB, that I knew I had to have the ablation done, as soon as possible. So, luckily, I had it done. After that, those kinds of procedures weren't done for a while.

Then the virus hit, and no one went anywhere. I never went back to my daughters. After about two months we met halfway and had an outside visit.

Then, eventually she came to visit with the kids. She told me in May, they were moving to Canada. I was shocked and so saddened.

I remember a long time ago, a girlfriend was moving to Ohio. She was going with her three children and husband, to a better life in Ohio. They couldn't make it on the husband's salary in Long Island. She described how dramatic her mother-in-law reacted about her taking the kids away from her. With all her dramatics, it didn't stop them from going, she just made everyone feel bad. They wanted to avoid her. I didn't want to be her so there were no dramatics from me.

Maybe the middle class accepts their children moving away more, than the lower class. The middle and upper class seem to understand you have to move, sometimes for a better life. Where you were born may not be the best place for the rest of your life.

My sister was in Seattle, with her children, recuperating from a bad bout of cancer. Thank God, she recovered and wanted to come back to Florida, as soon as she was well enough.

I still had my husband. At this time, he is quite frail, can't walk too far and has episodes of confusion. It's hard to go out with him. I never know if he is going to be able to walk or just get dizzy and fall. He seems to be able to function at home but he can't do much.

I am frail myself but I still have some life left in me. I have to make my life worth living. As the cliché goes, I had to make lemonade out of lemons. I had to think, OK my daughter is going to Canada, my son may stay in the Netherlands, for a while. Let's look at the positive side of it. They are great places to visit in the summer to get away from the Florida summer heat. I had to be the palm tree that bends in the hurricane and lives. Not the mighty oak that doesn't bend in the hurricanes, breaks, and dies.

Everything I see, hear, or do, reminds me of something in my life. I try not to think about the past too much. I don't want to feel the things I regret in my life. I try to remember the good things. I try to think about the good in every situation of my life. No sense in thinking about a situation in a bad way. Even if it was bad, you have to find something good in it. I know this sounds morbid, but I wonder how I'm going to die. There are many ways you can die, if you are old. You can't pick the way, or time, you are going to die. Unless, you intend to commit suicide, which, few people do.

First, there is the quick way. This is my preferred way. I think most people's preferred way. You can die of a heart attack—just drop dead, very little pain then gone. This might happen to me. I do have heart problems. Then there is dying in your sleep. That sounds peaceful and not too upsetting.

The heart attack may happen in public and that might be difficult, for the people around. At least in your sleep, they may find you in a few days if you live alone or your partner will find you in the morning and be totally upset, because you are dead and they have been sleeping next to you; but only one person gets really freaked out.

Then there are some awful, quick ways; the unnatural, quick way—car accidents, airplane accidents, things such as that. You go quickly, but the few seconds before, are not what anyone wants to experience, quite unnatural. If you saw ghost movies, people who go that way, don't know they are gone. They come back and roam around as ghosts. Not good. I'm not talking about young men, going to war, and dying quickly. I'm just talking about old people dying quickly. I think dying in your sleep, or heart attacks are the best way to go.

Then, there are a host of long drawn out ways; some painful and others not painful to you but to the people around you. I think the worst is dying of cancer. Sometimes people linger in pain, for a long time wishing for death or having Hospice care, and know they are going to die; having nightmares about it. They usually are put on anxiety medicine to take away the stress of knowing they are going to die.

Then, there's the nursing home death. You get old, your mind is good but your body is failing, not from a devastating disease, such as cancer, but just little things slowly robbing you of your abilities. You first find you are very fragile then use a walker then a wheelchair. You have trouble using utensils and taking care of your personal needs but your mind is fine. Almost as bad as getting cancer; slow death.

Then, there is the loss of the mind. You start to forget things. Finally, you can't live on your own anymore, because you are doing dangerous things, such as leaving the stove on. So you are put in a nursing home but soon, you forget everything and everyone. Hopefully, you are in your own little happy world. You don't understand anything, including death. So you are happy. Your family may not be happy, in that you don't recognize them anymore and they are paying the big nursing home bill. I guess if I had to have a long drawn out death, this would be the easiest for me.

Women often outlive men. So women are the ones who live alone in their old age. I can see this happening to me. My husband is a much frailer than I am. Unless I go quickly from a heart attack, I'm probably going to outlive him and wind up living alone. Most women stay in the house for a few years then move to a condo or an apartment. They can't keep up the house themselves.

Many older women live here in Florida; their children and families live elsewhere. As you get older, you must live where your body works the best. Most older bodies can't take the cold, ice and snow, even if all their family lives in the same spot. If it's cold, you can't move near them for health reasons. No sense in trying, you can find yourself getting sick and just being a burden, not enjoying your life and probably making others' lives miserable. So, you can't just up and leave and go near your children, even if they want you. The lower class usually doesn't have this problem. They never moved in the first place. So the older people just stay where they are and become shut-ins if they live in a cold area.

Memories

I have an image of what the perfect old age is. It's living near both my children, seeing my grandchildren all the time. Having big family holidays together, just being around all my family and friends; I have to get this image out of my head. There is no perfect old age. There is only what you have and you have to make that as perfect as possible.

I once saw a movie, about this older woman, who lives in a condo down in Florida. She is alone, and decides to take dancing lessons, to do something. This gay guy comes, and gives her dance lessons. They become friends, and at the end, when she gets cancer, he is the one that helps her—sad story but not so farfetched.

There is a saying some old person made, about the young generation. He said he is worried about the future of the world, because the younger generation didn't know what they were doing. This was said by a philosopher, in the middle ages. I guess every older generation, thinks the younger generation, doesn't know what they are doing but the world still seems to be here.

Some acceptance, understanding, and peace, comes with old age. I learned the world seemed to go on. No matter who was the president, what catastrophes hit the earth, it still seemed to continue its orbit. When I was younger, I would argue with people about politics, especially about the president. I don't anymore. If you have different points of view, it only causes anger between each of you; not good, party conversations, not good conversation for a good time or anytime. In all my years, the earth, and the United States, didn't end, because there was a president in office, for whom I didn't vote. Somehow everyone lived on no matter what happened, no matter who was president.

The main thing is to make sure the younger generation survives, especially when they are children. Go back to the basic needs, food, sleep, shelter, security, and love. Make sure your family has those basic things. Take care of your family first, especially the children.

There is a saying: everything I needed to know about life, I learned in kindergarten. This can be true. In kindergarten you learn to share, accept others, not talk about others, you learned to play and work well, with everyone. You couldn't take anyone else's belongings. You weren't allowed to talk nasty, fight or hit anyone. You learn to protect yourself and stick up for your rights, without being the bully. You learned to follow the rules; you had respect for the teacher, the authority figure. You learned to go and talk to the teacher, if something was wrong and work it out. You learned how to defend yourself. You learned how important it was, to come home and relax and have the support and love of your family and friends. You learned how wonderful and important it was to have someone who loved you and someone to love back.

As a child, I lived in the Projects. I used to see these poor little old ladies, sitting by their window, looking out their project windows. Not having anything to do. They seemed lonely and unhappy. I said, "Please God, don't let me wind up the same as them." My prayer was answered.

About the Author

Marianne earned her Master's degree in Reading education from Adelphi University and her Bachelor's Degree from Queens College in Elementary Education and Psychology. She has extensive teaching experience and has won the "Presidents' Club Award" from the International Reading Association for her work. She also received a Commendation from The City of Milpitas CA, for services to the community through displaying art at the Phantom Art Gallery. She was a Director of the Nassau Reading Council, and a member of the Wellington Art Society, Lake Worth Art League, The Authors Guild, and South Florida Writers.